Knockout Interview

Fourth edition

John Lees

 McGraw-Hill Professional

Knockout Interview
Fourth Edition
John Lees

ISBN-13: 9780077189563
ISBN-10: 0077189566
e-ISBN: 9780077189570

Published by McGraw-Hill Education
8th Floor, 338 Euston Road
London
NW1 3BH
UK

Telephone: +44(0) 20 3429 3400
Website: www.mheducation.co.uk

British Library Cataloguing in Publication Data
A catalogue record for this book is available from the British Library
Library of Congress Cataloguing in Publication Data

The Library of Congress data for this book
is available from the Library of Congress

Typeset by Transforma Pvt. Ltd., Chennai, India
Printed and bound by CPI Group (UK) Ltd, Croydon

First published 2003
Second edition published 2008
Third edition published 2012
First published in this fourth edition 2017

McGraw-Hill Education books are available at special quantity
discounts to use as premiums and sales promotions or for use in
corporate training programs. To contact a representative, please
email b2b@mheducation.com

Knockout Interview

PRAISE FOR *KNOCKOUT INTERVIEW*

"When I read John's writing, two things happen. First, I feel as if he's standing right there, personally advising me. And second, I always come away thinking over the issue in a new way. It's a rare, but very useful, gift."

Sarah Green, Associate Editor,
Harvard Business Review

"Knock your interviewer out with this insider's guide to landing the job you love! You have in your hands the wisdom of years of interviewing! Through 125 questions, John Lees takes you behind the scenes of the interview process from start to finish from the candidate, interviewer and organisation perspective. This guide offers you unique insights, practical tips, techniques and downloadable worksheets. So, the next time you walk into the 'ring' be sure you are prepared . . . with Knockout Interview."

Ajaz Hussein, International Career Counsellor

"A brilliant book which I wholeheartedly recommend to my coaching clients. John takes you step by step through every question you could face in an interview, from the deceptively simple, to some of the toughest. Not only will you learn how to answer them with ease, but also the reasons behind why they are being asked, allowing you to perform at your best and get the job. A must read for any job seeker."

James Curran, Career coach and podcast host
at www.graduatejobpodcast.com

"The old adage attributed to Benjamin Franklin of "By failing to prepare, you are preparing to fail" is never more apt than when applied to interviews. The top career strategist and author John Lees has followed up on his excellent series of books with another winner here. If you are anxious about an upcoming interview or want to improve your performance in the future, reading Knockout Interview will be an ideal solution. The 125 questions in the book cover almost any eventuality but are presented in a format that is much more than just a list. Each question is followed by excellent guidance on how to decode the question and structure your answer. *Knockout Interview* is as comprehensive a resource on succeeding at interviews as any on the market."

David Levinson, Careers Manager,
University of Glasgow

"John gives consistently good, pragmatic advice and provides suggestions to help people make the most of themselves and the opportunities they get. Easy to read, relevant and straightforward, the book offers so much more than standard self help books – it provides practical steps to get readers started and give them confidence to take ownership of their careers. A great resource to ensure a head start in a competitive market."

Denise Nesbitt, Senior Change Delivery
Manager, Talent & Development,
Lloyds Banking Group

"This book is a great source of information and advice for anyone approaching a job interview. By helping you to understand your own strengths in the context of your future employer's requirements, John Lees' suggestions will make sure you prepare effectively for any style of interview. A wealth of strategies to cover the questions that many candidates dread will help you to avoid the pitfalls and demonstrate why you are the right candidate, setting you on the path to the next stage in your career."

Gary Argent, Director of the Career and Skills Development Centre, City University London

"Once again, John shows how to be at your very best in front of a prospective employer. This latest edition covers every aspect of interview preparation and is a must read for anyone in job search. As ever, his advice is eminently practical and accessible, delivered in a caring and supportive voice that will resonate with all readers and encourage them to embrace every job search opportunity."

Sophie Rowan, Coaching Psychologist at Pinpoint, author of *Brilliant Career Coach*

PRAISE FOR *KNOCKOUT CV*

"A comprehensive and practical guide to building a relevant, evidence-based CV which will win the recruiter's attention. Looks afresh at the role of your CV, the pitfalls to avoid and shares invaluable recruiter insights."

Liz Mason, Associate Director, Alumni Career Services, London Business School

"You write a CV for a purpose – to get a job. *Knockout CV* works backwards from the desired result, analysing each feature of the CV from the perspective of impact on the decision-maker. No frills, no diversions, simply full of practical help."

Shirley Anderson, HR Director, Talent and Reward, Pilkington Group Limited

PRAISE FOR *HOW TO GET A JOB YOU LOVE*

"This book is a treasure. Read it, devour it, use it, and find that job you once dreamed about but had almost given up on."

Richard Nelson Bolles, author of
What Color Is Your Parachute?

"I frequently recommend job seekers or those at a career crossroads to read *How to Get a Job You Love* as it offers practical and easily accessible advice from someone with vast experience in the area."

Joëlle Warren, Managing Director,
Warren Partners Ltd

"A positive, practical and readable guide, packed with creative tools and common sense advice from an author who understands careers from all angles. This book will support and encourage you throughout your working life, from making your initial career decision to helping with long term career management. It will challenge your preconceptions of yourself and of the world of work, and help you to a more fulfilling career."

Julia Yates, Programme Leader,
MSc Career Coaching,
University of East London

"The popularity of John Lees' writing lies in his ability to connect with the sense many people have that they can be more than they currently are and deserve greater job satisfaction than they currently have. What makes his work distinctive is his use of his wide experience in careers coaching to provide tools and ways of thinking that any motivated individual can easily use to take control of their working life."

Carole Pemberton,
Career and Executive Coach, author of
Resilience: A practical guide for coaches

"I know first hand the joy that being in the right career can bring and I commend John Lees for his books and seminars which help other people do just that."

Rosemary Conley CBE

"Watch out – this book could turn your life upside down."

Liz Hall, Editor, Coaching At Work

"A thorough and insightful read, *Knockout Interview* covers every single step of the interview process. Knowing how important preparation is to a successful outcome, I would certainly recommend John's latest edition."

Mike Burgneay, Managing Director,
Chiumento Consulting Ltd.

This book is dedicated with love
and ever-increasing appreciation
to my parents, George and Mair Lees

Contents

Foreword by Kevin Green

An interview is still by far the most common selection method used by employers to decide who to hire. So, regardless of your skills, attitude and suitability, if you want to land your dream job you need to develop your interview capability. This book is a fantastic way to give yourself the best shot of getting the job you want.

At the Recruitment and Employment Confederation our members help candidates prepare for interviews every day of the year. The most important thing by far is to be fully prepared so you can show yourself in the best possible light. There is nothing worse than reflecting after an interview and hear yourself saying "if only".

The advice that's constantly given by REC agencies is to make sure you look the part – your appearance and body language are really important. First impressions count, so make sure yours is a positive one. Do research on the company, their competitors and even the person who will be interviewing you. By demonstrating your knowledge, you show that you're really interested in the company – this is often enough to make you stand out from the crowd.

The key area to focus on is answering questions. Start off by thinking about the questions you're likely to be asked. This book gives you over 125 to start with. Some are about your CV and experience to date, while others will be used to find out about your personality. Once you've identified typical questions, rehearse your answers. Ask others to use this book to ask you questions. You can't over-prepare – invest time in being as good as you can be.

John is an expert in this field and following the advice and guidance in this book will help you have the best chance of landing a great new role.

Happy reading and best of luck!

Kevin Green
Chief Executive
Recruitment and Employment Confederation

Preface

Job interviews are stressful. A conversation that may take little more than an hour can have a huge impact on your confidence and career future, yet too many people leave the results of job interviews to chance and instinct, hoping to improvise on the day and pluck answers out of the air. This book offers a shortcut to a rapidly improved interview performance.

Taking time to anticipate what will happen in an interview makes the difference between occasional knock-backs and repeated rejection. There are many aspects to preparation, and apart from giving example questions and answers, this book reveals the things you can do to get results: anticipating what an employer is looking for, thorough research, understanding your strengths, preparing lines of defence. Strong performers prepare for *every* kind of interview question – routine, difficult, probing, competency-based, skill-checking, or just plain off the wall.

This book draws on hard evidence of what employers and recruiters ask, and what they hear in your unguarded replies. This advice is designed to help you improve your interview performance in a tough marketplace where jobs may seem hard to find. You will find typical questions, understand why they're asked, and read sample answers to adapt to your circumstances. Insights into interview practice reflect today's demanding job market. This advice is designed to help you improve your interview performance in a tough marketplace, whatever kind of job you are chasing – public or private sector, mainstream employer or not-for-profit organisation.

The approach of this book is practical. There are no magic solutions on offer – no killer answers that guarantee a job offer. You're going to have to do some thinking and some work. You will learn what makes an interviewer tick, and the signals that set off alarm bells. You will learn how to cut out material and say the things that matter – taking care to be both coherent and memorable. You will learn how not to shoot yourself in the foot, and how to get past the toughest interview questions.

Don't just read the questions listed in this book – *use* them to develop and practise your answers until your interview performance reflects the best version of *you* that you are capable of delivering.

How to use this book if you have an interview TOMORROW

Twenty of the questions covered by this book are given a ✱ rating. You'll see this star symbol printed alongside key questions, and in the full list of questions (see page xxv).

These questions form an emergency resource kit if preparation time is limited, but they are also the main questions to prepare for in any interview. If you don't read anything else, you'll still have an advantage.

One quick tip: don't discuss pay until you've read the suggested answers to **Question 124 What sort of pay figure did you have in mind?** (see page 229).

About the author

John Lees is one of the UK's best known career strategists and the author of a wide range of business titles. *How to Get a Job You Love* regularly tops the list as the bestselling career change handbook by a British author and has twice been selected as W H Smith's 'Business Book of the Month'. His books have been translated into Arabic, Georgian, Polish and Spanish. He is a regular blog contributor to *Harvard Business Review* online and, in 2012, wrote the introduction to the *HBR Guide to Getting the Right Job*.

John appears frequently in the national press and his work has been profiled in *Management Today*, *Psychologies*, *Coaching at Work* and *The Sunday Times*. On TV he has contributed to the BBC interactive *Back to Work* series programme, BBC2's *Working Lunch*, Channel 4's *Dispatches*, Sky News, and ITV's *Tonight – How to Get a Job*. He has delivered career workshops in Australia, Germany, Ireland, New Zealand, Mauritius, South Africa, Switzerland and several parts of the USA.

John is a graduate of the universities of Cambridge, London and Liverpool, and has spent most of his career focusing on the world of work, spending 25 years training recruitment specialists. He is the former

Chief Executive of the Institute of Employment Consultants (now the IRP). He has consulted for a wide range of organisations including: British Gas Commercial, The British Council, CIPD, Gumtree, Harrods, Hiscox, The House of Commons, Imperial College, The Association of MBAs, Lloyds Banking Group, Marks & Spencer, NAPP Pharmaceutical, National Audit Office, Oakridge, Standard Life, plus business schools across the UK.

John is a Fellow of the CIPD, an Honorary Fellow of the Institute of Recruitment Professionals, an NICEC Fellow, and was a founding Board Director of the Career Development Institute (CDI).

Alongside his day job, John serves as an ordained Anglican priest in the Diocese of Exeter. John is married to the poet and children's writer Jan Dean. They live in East Devon.

w: www. johnleescareers.com
Tw: @JohnLeesCareers

John Lees Associates helps career changers across the UK, specialising in helping people to make difficult career decisions – difficult either because they don't know what to do next or because there are barriers in the way of success.

Other careers books by John Lees published by McGraw-Hill Education

Knockout CV (2013), £10.99, ISBN 0077152859
Building on an extensive review of what employers love and hate about CVs, this book helps you decide which CV format will work best for you. How to write CVs and cover letters that convey your strengths quickly and get you into the interview room.

How to Get a Job You Love (2016), £12.99,
ISBN 0077179544
The ninth edition of John Lees' definitive career book. A single volume career coaching programme designed to help everyone who has found themselves saying 'I want to do something different, but I don't know what it is'.

This book is a treasure. Read it, devour it, use it, and find that job you once dreamed about but had almost given up on.
Richard Nelson Bolles, author of '*What Color Is Your Parachute?*'

Career Reboot – 24 Tips for Tough Times (2009), £9.99, ISBN 9780077127589
Packed with quick-read, practical tips for rejuvenating your job search, this book is a must for anyone striking out into a difficult job market after redundancy or simply looking for new opportunities in a difficult market.

Take Control of Your Career (2006), £12.99,
ISBN 9780077109677
How to manage your career once you've got a job, learning how to read your organisation, avoid career traps, renegotiate your job role and enhance your future without losing control of your life balance.

Acknowledgements

With age comes, perhaps later than it should, a realisation of those many people I haven't thanked enough.

Thanks again to Matthew DeLuca, President of the Management Resource Group, Inc. of New York City, for many years ago allowing me to adapt his McGraw-Hill title *Best Answers to The 201 Most Frequently Asked Interview Questions*. Some of his original ideas still inform this book.

My special thanks go to Dick Bolles, author of the world-famous *What Color Is Your Parachute?* My work as a career strategist was inspired by the creativity, wisdom and generosity of 125 hours' teaching from Dick at two of his summer workshops in Bend, Oregon, and two decades of encouragement and support.

Thanks are also due more people than I can hope to remember who have guided my thinking on interviews. Many people have provided ideas, encouragement, or great questions over the years: Charlotte Ashley-Roberts, Gill Best, Jo Bond, Richard Braybrooke, Catherine Brooks, Julian Childs, Claire Coldwell, Hilary Dawson, Zena Everett, Peter Fennah, Helen Green, Peter Hawkins, Kathryn Jackson, Stuart Lindenfield, Stuart McIntosh, Brian McIvor, Rosemary McLean, Adi Mechen, Andy O'Hanlon, Amiel Osmaston, Bernard Pearce,

Carole Pemberton, Bill Pitcher, Daniel Porot, Rhymer Rigby, Stuart Robertson, Robin Rose, Sophie Rowan, Valerie Rowles, Sital Ruparelia, Denise Taylor, Joëlle Warren, Ian Webb, Richard Weston, John Whapham, Elie Williams, Janie Wilson, Ruth Winden, and Laura Woodward.

Special thanks go to Kate Howlett, Managing Consultant at John Lees Associates, for her wisdom and many insights into careers work. My warm thanks to to the McGraw-Hill team, especially James Heath, Marketing Manager, and my constantly enthusiastic editor, Monika Lee. Finally, my huge appreciation goes to my agent James Wills at Watson, Little, for his diligence and encouragement.

List of 125 questions

List of worksheets

More user-friendly, A4 versions of these worksheets can be downloaded from www.johnleescareers.com.

Simply register on the website free of charge, then look for these documents (title prefix 'KNOCKOUT INTERVIEW') in the free resources section of the members' area:

Understanding the world of job interviews

What's a job interview? Interestingly, that's a question no book ever needs to address. Even in a high-tech world nearly everyone from late childhood onwards knows what a job interview is and what it's for. It's the stock-in-trade of movies, cartoons, and comedy sketches. The archetypal cartoon shows a smartly dressed and overbearing interviewer and a harassed candidate.

We know a bit about what it feels like, too – from the perspective of a job applicant, at least. Play word association with 'job interview' and you quickly get 'nerves' and 'interrogation'. Less of us might think about the perspective of the interviewer, for whom the event can sometimes feel uninspiringly repetitive. Reading CVs and interviewing candidates comes relatively low on any HR Manager's list of preferred activities. Seeing this contrasting picture will help you understand how just a small amount of effort can make you an effective and memorable interviewee.

Interview handbooks often stress the idea that an interview is a two-way conversation – the interviewer decides if you fit the role, and you decide whether the organisation is right for you. That's a misunderstanding – perhaps one aimed at maintaining candidate dignity. *The purpose of a job interview is to solve a problem by putting someone into a job.* An interviewer's task is to decide as quickly as possible whether you're right for a job offer. Your task is to help – by providing the right information in the right way, and by showing how well you fit the role, the team, and the organisation. Your job is to make it easy for the interviewer to offer you the job.

That's it. You don't have to become an interview superstar, fake it, seduce, or schmooze. And you certainly shouldn't be using the interview to find out whether you really want the job – there are plenty of ways of doing that outside the interview room, as Chapter 13 will reveal.

The changing face of job interviews

Effective recruitment has been described as *the right person in the right time at the right cost.* Recruitment is expensive, and interviews are a major drain on staff time. So why do they happen? Essentially, because employers want to discover information that your CV doesn't provide.

Often jobseekers face an uphill struggle. Employers can take their pick from a highly talented field, with many graduates applying for relatively low-level positions. It's easy to feel downhearted if you experience repeated rejections. The Internet makes research easier, but it doesn't make job search quicker; the growth of the hidden job market means that fewer jobs are advertised, and more jobs are filled by informal connections – especially word of mouth. At times it's a buyers' market when employers raise the bar, holding out for candidates who match the role exactly. And yet, even when vacancies are rare, many employers still find it difficult to find staff with the right skills.

At the same time, they see too many candidates who have done minimal preparation for the interview, and have only the vaguest idea about how they match the job.

Even in the uncertain European marketplace which has followed the Brexit referendum vote, interviews are still the norm. New technology provides some shortcuts, but face-to-face interviews are still seen as good value. It's probably true that interviews are getting shorter, less exploratory, and shortlists getting smaller to reduce staff time. Interviewers have become more process-driven – less inclined to spend time getting to know candidates, and more reliant on technology or quick-fix processes such as online applications and telephone screening. However, interviews remain a vital stage in the process – it's rare to get a job offer without at least one face-to-face discussion. Instinctively, interviewers feel a need to meet people (with video a near-acceptable alternative). They want to get a sense of what you'd be like as a work colleague or sitting across the desk from a customer.

Candidates are learning that it now takes more effort and creativity to win interviews. They have to jump new hurdles, including online testing, telephone screening and Skype interviews (see Chapter 9). Making connections and building relationships matter more than ever – you are far more likely to be interviewed if something is known about you already. Managing the picture you create from the first time you contact an organisation is also critical when competition is high. In other words, working towards a job offer has become more complicated and requires a wider range of skills.

What else has changed? Jobs and organisations have become more complex, yet employers expect you to undertake thorough research and to match yourself against the role.

Even so, the good news is that smart preparation, rehearsal, and decoding the needs of an organisation are straightforward techniques that provide a significant advantage. A structured job search campaign, thorough research, attention to your interview performance (thinking about your overall impact, not just what you say), and smart anticipation of interview questions all help you move closer to an employer saying 'yes'.

Building towards a great interview technique

If you've got as far as a job interview you've already done well. You've demonstrated your ability to do the job. Now you need to stand out from a group whose skills and experience broadly match yours. Some of them may have done this exact job before. Some may be internal candidates already known to the organisation.

To get the job, being competent isn't enough. It's often said that a job offer doesn't go to the person best equipped to do the job, but to the candidate who gives the best interview performance. This doesn't mean that employers are easily hoodwinked by showy people, but reflects the limitation of most job interviews – they rely on inaccurate second-hand information. Yes, an interviewer can pick up a great deal about your working style and communication skills from talking to you, but most workplace skills will be described rather than shown in action. What you have done matters; how you explain it matters more.

So, an interview really is a performance – organised, anticipated, an event where you communicate rehearsed stories and planned messages. Although an interviewer will have a plan for the event it is also up to you to prepare this performance, ensuring that you get the best of yourself across without making the classic mistakes which push you off the shortlist (see the **Top 10 interview mistakes that will lose you the job** at the end of Chapter 5).

What a great performance looks like to a decision maker

What do top performing interviewees do differently? You might think they're immaculately cool under pressure, have perfectly rehearsed answers including a slick 'elevator pitch'. You might feel they are more articulate, have more charm or just better things to talk about. Think again. Ask employers what kind of people they give jobs to, and they talk about candidates who are easy to get on with and who provide well-prepared, relevant answers.

Interviewers report they enjoy meeting applicants who. . .

- Are easy to talk to and seem interested in building a relationship.
- Show that the interview is important – some anxiety is present, but also lots of preparation.
- Listen carefully to questions and make sure their answers match them.
- Plan for questions by preparing answers matching the key features of the role.
- Show enthusiasm for the role, and can say why they want it.
- Don't offer glib statements but describe their skills and know-how with quiet confidence. They show what experience has taught them.
- Prepare short, memorable examples which showcase their skills and motivation.

- Ask a handful of relevant questions about the job.
- Arrive on time, looking and sounding the part from the moment they walk into the building.

Look at this list again. Is there anything completely impossible for you? There will naturally be things to work on – but that's true for even the best candidates. That's why you're reading this book.

Why 'going for the practice' might not help

Going to interviews can feel like a series of experiments, learning from the questions that come up and how your material is received. Some candidates go to interviews for jobs they don't want, saying this is 'just for practice'. Think about the downside. You may not get an interview, but if you do, your lack of real enthusiasm for the role will show. The likely outcome will be rejection. Even if you said from the outset that you didn't want or need the job, this will still have an impact on confidence.

Don't use live interviews as your only method of improving interview skills. Seek opportunities to improve your techniques and self-awareness. Practise talking about yourself, and ask for feedback. Try out trickier answers on friends and colleagues. Road-test your answers on contacts with HR or recruitment experience. Don't just seek praise and reassurance, but ask listeners to summarise what they hear. So don't just ask 'How did I do?', ask 'What can you remember from what I said?' and 'What's the first impression I gave when I started answering questions?' Do everything you can to make sure you are close to the top of your game before going to a real job interview.

Making luck work in your favour

It intrigues me that so many people believe they cannot plan for interview questions. Some questions may catch you off balance (see Chapter 11), but about four out of five questions are entirely predictable once you've learned how to interrogate job content. Anticipating questions is step one. The second step is half-rehearsing answers, so you have a pretty good idea what you will say as you open your mouth. That's where the work of the interview takes place – not in the interview room, under pressure, but quietly in advance. People don't avoid the task of anticipating questions because they are lazy. Sometimes it's because they don't know how to decode the job (see Chapter 3). Often the real reason is anxiety – we don't want to visualise the interview. If you don't want to think about an experience, you just let it happen.

Too many candidates believe that interview success is about luck. You *can* be lucky if questions come up that are entirely comfortable, but that can also make you complacent – *too* assured. Relying on luck means the 'wing it when you get there' approach – a secure way to put in a below-average performance. Where candidates pay lip service to preparation, their underlying plan is to improvise answers under pressure. This is a high-risk strategy. This book shows you how to second-guess the process. When the first tough question is fired at you, you won't be surprised, and you will be ready with examples and with the right details – so your reply will be clear, confident, and to the point. The old saying applies: 'The harder I work, the luckier I get.' Luck improves with effort and practice.

Improving the odds in your favour begins by digging deep so you really understand the employer's shopping list. Most interviews only give you a chance to showcase a couple of dozen pieces of information. How many of those allow an interviewer to tick a box on the job checklist? How many of your answers are predictable, 'vanilla', instantly forgettable? Start working on new material. This might look like hard work, but in fact we're talking about a commitment of a few hours – in pursuit of a job that could change the whole direction of your career.

Questions, questions. . .

Review the list of sample questions covered by this book (page xxv). There are 125 typical, likely interview questions – with supporting commentary and a range of example answers. Here's your first batch:

Q1   Did you have any problems finding us?

This question sounds like gentle chat, but the way you answer will prompt judgements about your working style. How do you come across? (Friendly, stand-offish, loud, inaudible?) What kind of interviewee are you? (Difficult, negative, irritable, open?) Plan for small talk, whether it takes place in the corridor or in the interview room itself. When you answer, speak clearly and at a good volume. Keep it positive – if you start by complaining, even about the weather, you start on a negative note:

'I had terrible problems parking – I wish you'd told me I would need change for the pay and display.'

Answers that give interviewers no cause for concern tend to be mildly upbeat and uncomplicated. Affirm that everything has gone smoothly so far (if things haven't, why mention it?) and your opening answer will instantly show **three great job qualities** – you're decisive, focused on essentials, and good at seeing the positive side of things:

'Not at all – very clear directions.'

Q2   What do you prefer to be called?

This question is a polite way of checking that it's okay to use your first name, and making sure that the interviewer gets it right. It helps if you type your name at the end of your covering letter in the way you prefer: if you're 'Christopher' on your passport but everyone calls you 'Kit', make that clear. If you really prefer a different version to the name the interviewer is using, mention it simply, but don't sound fussy or pedantic:

'Chris is fine.'

Q3   Can we offer you tea, coffee, a glass of water?

Accept the offer if you're waiting in reception, but decline in the interview room itself. Your hands may already be trembling and now you have to manage a cup or glass as well as your papers. If you really are too parched to speak, ask for a glass of water, take a good sip, then put it down somewhere you won't knock it over. If your mouth goes bone dry when you are nervous, eat a hard sweet or drink sugary black coffee before the interview – these are better than plain water.

Q4   What do you enjoy doing outside work?

Your interests may come into focus early, especially if you've mentioned them in a CV. The topic is often seen as a useful ice-breaker. Some interviewers want to find out if you are a 'rounded' person. Think carefully about what declared interests say about you. Are you active (*'avid runner'*) or passive (*'spectator'*), a reflective individual (*'write poetry'*) or an active joiner-in (*'Round Table'*)?

Whatever you list under 'interests', make sure that they are either relevant to the job or something you can talk about enthusiastically if pushed. Don't claim interests just because they sound good – a knowledgeable interviewer can undermine these claims in seconds. So, don't put 'reading' unless you've just finished a book worth talking about, and don't put 'keeping fit' if your gym membership expired last winter. If you are perceived to be dishonest on this point, your work history will also seem inauthentic. Don't mention too many interests because that may imply that work takes second place in your life.

Interests are far more likely to come up if your work experience is limited. If you hit on something an interviewer finds interesting, it's more likely you'll be remembered. This topic can provide you with a great opportunity to talk about motivation and skills. For example, a hobby might have helped you develop research or organisational skills. Show you actively chose an interest rather than drifting into it, and mention skills and qualities that matter to your next employer:

'I've been learning the tango for a few years now, and it's still a challenge, but it really makes you focus – and it's a great way to meet fascinating people.'

✷Q5   Tell us about yourself

This apparently simple question is one of the toughest you will face. The problem is that you have no frame of reference. Should you use a one-line summary? Should you talk in detail about your work experience or your skills? The question might come at the beginning of an interview (and may even be used to throw you off balance just a little). The trap too many candidates fall into is to give a long-winded summary of their work history. Possible reasons an interviewer might ask this question include:

- The interviewer hasn't had a chance to read your CV.
- It's a deliberately broad question just to see what you will come up with.
- It's a very general opener encouraging you to give a brief overview of your background.
- It's a question seeking evidence of your personality.

Sometimes the question will be specific: 'Tell me about your career, starting with school, and progressing through the jobs that you have held.' Even in this scenario, keep things brief. Your answer should last **no more than two or three minutes**, otherwise you lose the interviewer's attention. Plan a short script – your first **Safety Zone Response** (see page 91). Get your message across in two or three short sentences, and then quietly wait for a response – the interviewer will either move on or say if more is required. Here are some sample answers for different scenarios.

- **If you are re-entering the job market after time out:** *'I have experience in both the third sector and commercial environments, primarily managing information. I've been away from salaried positions during the past few years to focus* *on my family, but even so I have been involved in a number of community-based projects that have enhanced my business skills and given me a good range of contacts.'*

- **Where you are looking to make a move up the ladder:** *'After starting as a management trainee, I enjoyed the chance to manage my own team. I'm looking now for a chance to broaden my management skills in a larger organisation. . .'*
- **Where you want to make a career change:** *'After achieving my degree in engineering I very much enjoyed the opportunity to work in the utilities sector, with a strong emphasis on infrastructure. That has shown me that what I am really interested in is broader project management work, which is why I am now looking at construction companies. . .'*

Q6   What prompted you to apply for this role?

This question is a great opportunity to make a positive first impression. Remember the one message an employer does *not* want to hear – *'I was looking for a job and this came up'*, or, even worse, *'I need a job, and this will do for the moment.'* A question like this is essentially looking at four key areas:

- The kind of job you're looking for. (See also **Q8** and **Q36**.)
- What do you find interesting about this organisation? (See **Q21**.)
- How clear are you about what you're looking for? (See **Q65**.)
- How sure are you that you match what we're looking for? (See **Q52**.)

Whatever you say, begin with enthusiasm, moving on to offer a quick match between what you're looking for and what's on offer:

'I was really excited to see this position advertised. I've been in L&D for five years now, designing courses and developing a wide range of learning materials, but this role would be a great step up for me because of the opportunity to develop a full range of intranet resources.'

Q7 Why did you leave your last position?

Interviewers are always curious about reasons for job change. Do you let circumstances decide your fate, or do you choose when to move on? Do you drift from job to job? Was your last employer glad to get rid of you? These scenarios are running through the interviewer's mind. If you have stated a reason in your cover letter or in conversations with a recruitment consultancy, be consistent in your interview answer. Summarise quickly without lingering over any sense of disappointment or resentment:

'I realised the best way to move on was to call it a day and focus on finding a new role, creating space and time to do some active networking that I couldn't do while holding down a full-time job.'

'I was made redundant last June. The first three months were tied up taking a refresher course in accounting. Since then I've focused on making good connections to spot roles before they're advertised. . .'

Be clear about your motivation for the changes you have made, and how they fit your career plan:

'I always intended to work for just three or four years in marketing to give me a better insight into that part

of the business, but my long-term aim has been to move into a general management role. . .'

If you were formally dismissed from your last job, you may have to disclose this. Take professional advice about what you should disclose in an interview or on an application form. Don't lie, but don't leave what you say to chance. Talk about what you learned from the experience. This answer will never be easy, but you can make the best of a bad situation:

'I was dismissed from the role, formally on performance issues, but we all recognised that the relationship wasn't working. I've done a lot of thinking since then and I know now where things went wrong and what kind of role would work best for me. . .'

If you left on a compromise agreement this is usually confidential so you don't need to supply details beyond a short statement:

'I realised it was time to move on because it was clear that we had too narrow a skill set in my team. I agreed and negotiated an exit package so I could find a role where those skills were in demand.'

Another situation is where your contract was not extended beyond a probationary period. Disclose facts carefully, demonstrating a firm conviction that you learned something from the experience. Be certain that your version is corroborated by a former employer if a reference is taken:

'I was asked to leave at the end of my three-month probationary period because my boss said he felt threatened by having someone more experienced

than him as his number two. He was very apologetic and straightforward about it, and helped me to find a new job.'

Q8   What kind of job are you looking for?

This is a big question, often asked at an early stage, sometimes during a telephone screening interview. It's a question which captures your motivation, your clarity of thought, and your career intentions, so don't duck it or hope it won't come up.

If someone asked you this question over coffee, you would probably mention job titles, but naming specific jobs can limit your options. Talk about the main components in your ideal job mix, relating them closely to the opportunity on offer:

'My background is ten years in financial services with a strong emphasis on the customer experience. I'm looking for a role where I can use this knowledge in the hospitality or entertainment sectors.'

'The reason I'm excited about this job is that I'm looking for a role where I can draw on my design skills but also spend more time talking to end users.'

Q9   Why can't I find you on LinkedIn?

Tough questions can come up right at the start of an interview. If you have any kind of social media presence, assume that an employer has access to some or all of the information you post about yourself online. Unless you are unusually guarded in your privacy settings, material is out there. Try searching your name in Google and see how long it takes to find yourself – and look carefully at what comes up.

Restrict personal information to friends and close contacts, and maintain a more public space for your job search activity. In practice this means setting up a LinkedIn page, and most recruiting organisations will be looking for this electronic 'shop window'. Selectors want to see how you describe yourself in your profile, and employers may also check your work and study history. They may also be interested in your connections and the discussion forums where you make contributions. At interview you may be asked about information on LinkedIn you haven't supplied in your CV.

What if you're not on LinkedIn? It's not compulsory, and for some roles it won't make much difference. However, if the role requires you to be media savvy, the absence of an up-to-date profile suggests you don't know how to handle social media, or you don't care. Neither may be true, but it's what an employer assumes from absent information. It's almost as damaging to have a profile with almost zero content and only two or three connections (that says you've tinkered but not taken a real interest).

Top 10 'start-up' tips

1. **Begin by browsing** through the book. Pick out the questions you know are most relevant to you, and the questions you will find it most difficult to answer. Start preparing your response.
2. **Plan your time** and use it effectively, particularly if you are unemployed. Get support from friends, colleagues, and groups designed to assist job searchers. Commit to spend about twice as much time on your job search than you were planning to when you bought this book.

3. **Pick out questions** in the book that worry you the most. Start to sketch out answers on paper before finding a colleague to practise with.

4. **Gather evidence**: Many questions will require you to have evidence at your fingertips, so start to review your work history.

5. **Start cataloguing**: Write in the book. Complete the exercises and keep a record of your discoveries.

6. **Focus on preparation** – yourself, your evidence, and your homework on the organisation.

7. **Focus on your strengths**: Do not get stuck criticising yourself, but examine your behaviours and accentuate the positives.

8. **Enjoy the interview process** – meeting people and learning about different organisations.

9. **Learn from each interview**: Whether you were offered the job or not, use each interview experience as a laboratory to develop better techniques and better answers.

10. **Prepare for rejection**: You'll get knock-backs – everyone does. Accept the fact that a proportion of interviews may be unsuccessful. Pick yourself up, cheer yourself up – but don't commit to a major change of strategy when you are at your lowest ebb (see Chapter 13).

2 | The secrets of interview preparation

Your next interview is approaching. How are you going to prepare for it? That may seem like a question with an obvious answer. However, every day employers comment on the fact that interviewees seem to have undertaken only minimal preparation.

Areas where candidates frequently under-prepare

1. Doing basic homework about the nature, history and style of the organisation.
2. Looking in detail at job content and anticipating the key skills required.
3. Anticipating questions which are likely to come up.
4. Thinking about what the organisation needs.
5. Finding stories from their experience to match the role.

Some items on this list appear very straightforward. For example, ticking the first item off your list can take less than an hour. Nothing in the list is surprising or difficult. So why don't people prepare better? One reason is that items 2–5 in the above list require a little experience of decoding jobs and organisations (see Chapter 3). However, the main reason people don't prepare is that they *choose not to*. They think that they can improvise answers on the spot. They think that an interview is a relatively dull process not worth planning for. They believe it's the interviewer's job to make things go well. Or they don't prepare because imagining the interview makes them feel anxious.

The fear factor

Only the last objection in this list makes sense. Under pressure you may find that you don't hear questions properly, and you can't remember evidence. Interview nerves are to be taken seriously, but you do nothing for *future* interview nerves by deliberately setting yourself up to fail. That's what under-preparation is – a secret unspoken agreement that you're going to wreck your chances of getting an offer. Your future confidence will not be improved by putting yourself into events where under-preparation is going to be visible and obvious – leading to predictable rejection.

So, stress often leads to avoidance – not preparing for the interview because you can't bear to imagine it. Look instead at the positive effects of anxiety on your performance. Elevated response levels help you give the event the attention it deserves. You can even get to enjoy the adrenalin rush, particularly if you're ready. Being prepared turns fear into focus.

Don't make the same mistakes as the average job-seeker who says '*I don't know what they'll ask me, so I will think of something on the spot.*' Imagine you were advising someone making an important presentation to senior staff. Would you say 'Wing it – just make it up when you get there'? Of course not. You'd talk about content, style, impact and preparation. Preparation makes interviews much, much easier. You've done the work of the interview well before you get in the room.

Setting goals

Someone might say 'good luck' to you before a job interview. If that boosts your confidence, great – but push the odds in your favour by thinking about goals.

YOUR THREE BASIC INTERVIEW GOALS

Goal 1: Be easy to talk to. Your first goal is to practise your technique of being an interview candidate. Learn how to relax enough so you appear at ease. Try small talk to reassure the interviewer that things are going well. Listen carefully to questions, and answer concisely, allowing space and time for the interviewer's schedule. All this requires practice, not instinct.

Goal 2: Cover the ground. Your second goal is to get across the right amount of relevant information – your best stories matched against the key requirements of the job. Talking too much means you may miss part of the target. Keep a picture of the job in mind to ensure you cover everything you think is important.

Goal 3: Show you fit the part. Your final goal is to send a clear message that you're a natural fit for the role and a good team member. This is the impression you create from the moment you step into the building. An interview is an audition for a part you hope to play.

Goals 1 and 2 above are within your control from the outset. If you know you have strong evidence matching role requirements, communicate it – even if the right question fails to come up. Take responsibility for Goal 1 – whatever kind of interviewer you get, make the conversation go well. For Goal 2, decode (see Chapter 3). If Goal 2 troubles you, think. If you don't have the right skills or experience, are you wasting your energy on random job applications? Goal 3 is more problematic – it's not always easy to make the chemistry of an interview work, and there may be other candidates whose personality offers a better fit. Even so, do everything you can to achieve Goals 1–3, *every time.*

Understanding yourself and your 'offer'

Complete the **Interview Preparation Sheet** below to catalogue useful and relevant information about yourself (this is useful for your CV as well as for preparing interview answers).

This worksheet covers the key parts of your offer. It concludes with your background knowledge. Later in the chapter we'll see how you say useful things about your studies and qualifications. First we deal with one of the main items on any employer's shopping list.

Skills

When you were completing the **Interview Preparation tion Sheet**, did you find it difficult to list your skills? One problem is that when we're asked about our skills, we either talk about the job we currently occupy, or the skills which we think might be relevant to our next employer. Many job changers only see half the picture when it comes to their own skill set. Sometimes they don't know what their skills are, and at other times they only see skills which other people value.

Skills are about what you *do*, the activities that fill your working day. Skills draw upon personality characteristics and underpinning knowledge, but they're fairly simple items. Often a great way to think about your skills

Interview Preparation Sheet
What I can do: List the skills that you regularly use under the headings provided.

Skills I use around **people**	Skills I use with **technical problems**
Skills I use requiring **imagination and creativity**	Skills I use requiring **analysis and organisation**
Skills I use to solve **practical problems**	Skills I regularly use **outside work**

HOW I use these skills: List words that others have used to describe your working style (for example, cheerful, resourceful, creative, loyal, methodical. . .).
WHERE I have used these skills: Record details of roles and projects.
What I know: List any areas where you have particular knowledge or expertise. Start with your studies, but look at areas of work where you have acquired specialist knowledge.

is to imagine someone spending a month shadowing you at work with a video camera. If you watched that footage you'd see what you *do* most of the time – how much time you spend looking at screens, working with other people, on the telephone, or out and about.

Look in detail at past jobs, and think about the skills that were required, the skills you brought to the role, and the skills you learned. Which skills do you use particularly well? What do you have in your skill set which other people don't have? Most importantly of all, think about the **evidence** that you have to support any statement you might have about skills. Take along a portfolio containing visual evidence of your work if that's useful. Sometimes it's good to have a relevant press cutting with you or a copy of a letter from a happy customer. It's usually enough to talk about appraisals, praise from managers, or customer feedback – you probably won't need hard evidence to hand. At a later stage in the process you might need to provide documentary evidence of past study, training, qualifications, and awards.

Transferable skills

The phrase 'transferable skills' is one you hear widely. It's clearly true that skills we learn in one job can also be used in another, sometimes even if the job is in a completely different sector. However, even experienced candidates fail to see that employers prefer to hear about skills which match the role exactly. People make recruitment decisions under pressure, and they don't have time to join the dots. So it's no use expecting an employer to work out how some of your skills might transfer. Your skills only start to become transferable when you translate them into language an employer not only *understands* but *can get excited about.*

You only decode that language by thoroughly investigating target employers well before an interview, which means understanding the language they use. There are several examples in this book of showing how skills are transferable (e.g. **Q12**, **Q52**, and **Q65**).

Naming, framing, and measuring your skills

As you prepare to answer interview questions, you might also want to think about how these answers will be tested. Here's a three-step approach to improving skill information:

1. **Name** the skill. Think about the words you use to describe each of your skills. Look at other jobs in the organisation and the language used in job advertisements to make sure that the skills you name make sense to the interviewer. For example, 'managing stakeholders' might be very meaningful language in one sector and in another might signal your unsuitability.
2. **Frame** the skill. Set the scene by providing details about the context – where were you using the skill? What problem were you trying to solve?
3. **Measure** the skill. How expertly do you use this skill? This is often made clear by giving an example of where you used a skill at the highest level.

Questions about your work experience and skills

Q10   Tell me about your current role

Interviewers often start with a question which is relatively easy to answer. This one seeks information

Analysing and presenting your skills

For more on skill discovery, see *How to Get a Job You Love*. If you are unclear of your motivated skills and how to communicate them, try the **JLA Skill Cards**. The skill cards come with a full set of instructions to help you identify your top ten skills and learn how to communicate them during job interviews. See **www.johnleescareers.com** for details.

about your most recent work. It's important not to get bogged down in a long answer, especially near the beginning of an interview. Many candidates provide excessive detail – a regurgitated job description. Instead, prepare a punchy summary which offers two or three messages about your strengths:

'It's been great working in a customer service role. It's a good team, and we've achieved some great results.

I really enjoy dealing with customers and coming up with different ways of solving their problems. But I think it's time to move on into a role with greater responsibility.'

'My job is all about organising and retrieving data to meet the needs of internal customers. Most of the data requests are routine, but what I really enjoy doing is working closely with clients and creating the kind of customised reports you produce here.'

You may also be asked to describe a typical day at work, particularly if someone is unfamiliar with the role. Use your **Experience Catalogue** (page 72) in advance to pick up the major elements you want to talk about, even if they are not done on a daily basis. The interviewer doesn't need microscopic detail, so don't begin *'I start by making myself a cuppa at 8.30.'* Describe competencies which show your level of responsibility or skill, and those that match tasks in the job you're chasing.

'In a nutshell, my role is to log in all the day's jobs and allocate them to other staff members, handling any queries or problems they have. The rest of the day is spent making sure work is on schedule – plus, of course, dealing with additional one-off requests that come into the department. May I ask how that compares to the work flow in this role?

Q11 How did your job fit into the organisation?

With this question you'll probably start visualising an organisational chart in your head. Perhaps you reach for a pen to draw it. Stop. Think. How much does an

interviewer really want to know? The key issues are
these:

- How senior was your role – what was your actual
  responsibility?
- How senior was your boss?
- What part of the organisation were you working in?

*'I was responsible to the assistant secretary, which in
this organisation is equivalent to a departmental
head. I was responsible for a team of 15 staff, including
four team leaders.'*

Point out useful parallels between past jobs and the
organisation you're talking to:

*'With the last two foreign banks that I worked at I
became very flexible about frequent changes in senior
management. I found one key to my success was to
remain non-political and to build relationships with
new senior staff quickly.'*

★Q12   Talk me through your work history. . .

This question might seem odd, since this information is
in your CV. It might be asked because the interviewer
has only skim-read your details, but the usual reason
is that someone wants to hear how you make connections between different work experiences – and to
know if you've taken control of your career. Your body
language and vocal energy will also convey high and
low points. All this helps an interviewer understand
whether the role on offer makes sense.

Talk through your history, but summarise it. You might
say *'I'll be happy to talk about this in more detail later.'*

Briefly outline the roles you have held and the sectors you've worked in. Don't repeat the phrases used in your CV – use new terms to make your work history sound fresh and interesting. Prepare short and clear answers dealing with obvious gaps in your work history.

Try to describe your history so it has an understandable 'shape' (you might talk about what your roles have in common, and what you've learned). Second, get across two or three strong points about why you are a good match to the role:

'I think there's a thread that links all the jobs that I've done, and it's an interest in developing people. I started my working life as a lecturer, but then moved through a series of commercial training roles. More recently I've managed a training department and commissioned a number of major new projects. Would you like me to tell you more about that?'

Making your studies relevant

Many candidates make a big thing of educational qualifications in a job application. Your academic history may be less of a door-opener than you think; employers are generally more influenced by evidence of skills and achievement. Employers have only a passing interest in your study history, but they do want to know you have the intellectual capacity required by the job – and that you pick things up quickly.

If you qualified recently, you need to communicate why you chose a particular course, and any spin-off learning relevant to the job. If you have studied something which doesn't *appear* to relate to your chosen career path, you need a brief **Safety Zone Response** (see Chapter 6) to make relevant connections. Some candidates seem overqualified (see **Q15**). If you lack specified qualifications, offer compensating evidence (**Q16**).

If you qualified some time ago, an interviewer is going to wonder if you have kept up your learning, and what you have done in terms of continuous professional development (CPD). Remember that this includes attending conferences and seminars, reading articles, online learning, following blogs, and networking with fellow professionals. Demonstrate that you have made tangible efforts to keep skills and knowledge up to date.

List the areas of knowledge which seem necessary for the position you are applying for. Next, match them against your own learning history. Remind yourself of where and when you acquired know-how. Knowledge, of course, is not limited to classroom learning; so remind yourself of 'hidden' knowledge. For example, you may have knowledge of accounting software because you're treasurer for a charity. Don't miss out on-the-job training, seminars, or workshops you have attended (especially those which did not lead to certification, which you may have missed off your CV). Look again at all the night classes, distance-learning courses, and books you read *just to learn things for the sake of learning*.

Talking about your study history can be a smart way of subtly bringing employable skills into the discussion. Many academic courses provide students with skills they rarely talk about, even though they are attractive to employers:

- Researching a subject in depth.
- Analysing, processing, and checking information.
- Exploiting information technology.
- Teamworking.

- Organising events.
- Community involvement.
- Motivating yourself towards difficult goals.
- Managing your own time and workload.
- Making contacts with people and organisations.
- Influencing and persuading.
- Presenting information and ideas in writing or to an audience.

Q13 Why did you study that subject?

Any question that includes the word 'Why?' challenges the way you make decisions. A throwaway: *'It seemed a good idea at the time'* is dangerous. Worse still: *'I thought I would enjoy it, but. . .'*

Be ready with a short, positive answer that indicates that you thought about subject choice carefully and you found your studies interesting and useful. Even the suggestion that you chose the wrong subject is disturbing to the interviewer, because it communicates confusion about career objectives. You may be uncertain, but it does your cause no good to share this:

'The reason I chose economics was that I was fascinated by the subject and believed that it would equip me with a better understanding of the way businesses operate.'

You may be asked what you enjoyed about your studies. What you should hear is 'How was it relevant to the world of work?' (see **Q14**). Don't assume an interviewer will understand or value your qualifications. It's your job to communicate their relevance. Employers are not too interested in your choice of subject, but interested in outcomes – what can you do now that you couldn't before?

'What I really enjoyed most in my studies was writing a dissertation on my favourite author. This involved tracking down all kinds of things, and I learned how to organise information and resources for myself. I was even able to persuade this busy international writer to give me an interview, which I think demonstrates tenacity and powers of persuasion!'

'It taught me to absorb ideas quickly and communicate them in a language that is readily accessible. . .'

If you are not practising in the field that you studied (for example, you studied law but don't work as a lawyer), make it clear that you have moved in a conscious direction rather than recovering from failure to continue in your first choice of profession:

'Although I did get a law degree, it was never my intention to train as a solicitor. I felt that a legal background combined with my facility with language would uniquely prepare me for an international role.'

Even if your studies don't seem immediately relevant to the job, talk about other skills you used during your studies – for example, working in a team, organising projects, managing your workload, meeting deadlines.

'Essentially it's a degree which mixes economics and history, but the main thing is that it showed me how to research things in great detail by tracking down difficult and obscure information, and making connections across a wide range of information. For example, I undertook a project looking at the factors that make smaller organisations become large businesses. . .'

★Q14 How is your qualification relevant to this job?

This builds on the previous questions, and will be tricky to handle unless you are prepared. Don't assume that you will have done nothing of interest. The interviewer may only have a sketchy idea of what your academic subject covers, and will certainly be keen to hear you explain how skills you have acquired will be useful in the workplace. Identify one or two key areas in the job, and pick out matching areas of skill or knowledge from your studies (or from extracurricular activities):

'I can see how a degree in zoology may not seem like exactly the right qualification to get me into management consultancy. However, I believe that the function of a degree is really to teach you how to think, how to organise your own learning and manage your time so that you end up with a good degree without being excessively in debt.'

'In my final year I organised a field trip to Norway, using a number of organisational and planning skills which I think will be useful in this job.'

'As organiser of the year's largest charity ball I had my hands pretty full – and I learned a huge amount about booking facilities and entertainment, and how to feed 300 people and make a profit.'

Q15 What would you say if I suggested you're overqualified for this role?

Think yourself into the interviewer's shoes. Candidates who are overqualified may, in the eyes of a recruiter, be:

- **A problem** – you will want promotion quickly.
- Someone who will rapidly become **bored with the job** and move on quickly.

- A **know-it-all** who will make your boss's life hell.
- A **threat** who will challenge authority.
- **Desperate** to take any job at any salary.

If it's clear that the job you're looking at will be a step down, or that you will be much more qualified or experienced than others in the team, don't leave this issue unaddressed:

'Yes, on paper I will be more qualified than others in this department. However, I respect that people are a lot more experienced than me and I have a great deal to learn.'

Q16   Ideally, we wanted a graduate. . .

This question may present less of a barrier than you think. As explained above, employers only have a vague idea about how and why qualified people make better workers. Often there is a broad assumption that staff will do better if they have a good standard of education, or that graduates are more likely to have the intellect to cope with certain aspects of the job. Those without degrees often have alternative things to offer. First, they are often more experienced, having started their careers earlier. Second, if you can show you have skills, experience, and know-how at least as good as a graduate, that will often get you past this road block:

'I've worked alongside graduates in many stages in my career and I have often achieved promotion quicker than they did. I believe my track record shows I have the skills and knowledge you require for the role, and far more experience than a graduate my age.'

Q17   How do you keep informed professionally?

The question *assumes you keep informed profession-ally*, so prove it. Talk about conferences and learning events you have attended in the last two years. Think about publications and journals you regularly read, and also online discussion groups or blogs where you are a contributor. Whatever the sector, have at your fingertips:

- Key industry facts and figures.
- Trends in your sector.
- Key people in the industry.
- Major upsets and scandals.
- New theories, applications, and ideas.

'I make sure I get to a couple of good conferences every year, both to network and to keep learning. Two months ago I heard a great speaker. . .'

'I really enjoyed the team-building course I did this spring. It was well run, and gave me a huge number of insights into leading and motivating a team.'

'The job has been too pressured for me to attend any external training programmes, but I have personally led a number of in-house seminars. Teaching your colleagues means you really do have to do your homework. . .'

Q18   What prompted you to become an environmental engineer?

The occupational title here is of course infinitely variable – this is another question probing whether you are passive or active in your career decision-making. It also explores where your career is heading. The question is far more likely to be asked if your original training (to be an engineer, banker, chemist, teacher) is not directly related to the role on offer. Therefore, this question offers you a chance to sell yourself, perhaps as a candidate with a slightly unconventional background.

Here's another opportunity to explain your career story. Talk about the way you moved on from one area of work to another, but make it sound like an intelligent response to circumstances and opportunity. The important thing is to demonstrate that *you were always serious about your career* and that fact hasn't changed:

'Originally I was drawn to banking, and I had five really exciting years in the City. What I eventually realised was that I was much more interested in how people grow and learn, which is why I moved into learning and development. . .'

Personal preparation checklist

- Check the **location** of the interview. Plan your route carefully, perhaps even doing a 'dummy run' the day before if it's a really important interview.
- Telephone to double-check **arrival instructions** if you are uncertain of details: for example, you might want to find out if nearby car parks are likely to be full.
- Check the names and titles of **people** you are meeting, and ask reception how a name is pronounced if you are in doubt.
- Allow a big safety margin in terms of **arrival time**. Sit quietly in the car park or in a nearby café, and turn up at reception ten minutes before the interview is scheduled to take place, unless you are given more specific joining instructions. Arriving early will give you a chance to look around the area and the site, and talk to reception staff. Arriving late when it's your fault undoes all your preparation work.
- Take a copy of the **CV** and **cover letter** you used to win the interview, plus copies of the **job advertisement** and **job description**.
- On one side of A4 take along the highlights from your **research notes,** a note of any key messages you want to get across, plus the questions you've prepared for the end of the interview (see Chapter 12).
- Switch off your **mobile phone** before entering the building. Off, not silent. You don't need distractions or embarrassment.
- While waiting, 'warm up' through **small talk** with anyone you run across in the reception area. Get a feel for the culture of the organisation – is it formal, friendly, up to date? Do people look engaged and interested in their work? Look at the way the organisation values the interview itself. Is the interviewer on time and well-prepared?

3

Decoding the job

KNOWING HOW TO MATCH YOUR EVIDENCE

Ticking all the boxes

Many job-hunters read advertisements and job descriptions and then throw random information at employing organisations, some relevant, but much of it only vaguely related to the job. Better candidates know how to get under the surface of these documents and work out what the organisation is really looking for – before they try to supply matching evidence. So, if you're reading job details carefully and deciding which parts of your past will help your scorecard, you're making a good start.

Finding target organisations

Finding potential employers who may or may not be advertising jobs increases your chances of creating interview opportunities. Some desk research will help, and much of this can be done online. Find out the different ways of getting job boards to produce relevant, interesting vacancies in your geographical area. Advertised jobs may not be an exact match, but at least you know who is hiring. Develop an interest in employers so you pick up clues about why they might need new staff, such as growth, new products, high staff turnover, or a short-term gap. This preliminary research is critical – you're starting to understand the problems employers are trying to solve. Seek conversations with past or present workers, providing essential inside knowledge. When you have spotted organisations, find out more about them. Look at their websites to find out what sector they are in and what kinds of jobs they offer. It also pays to develop the habit of asking virtually everyone you meet *'Who should I be talking to?'*

Research can be hard work, especially when you hit setbacks – for example, when busy people don't return your call. Expect flat days. To keep your spirits up while researching, focus on organisations and sectors that you find exciting. This extra factor helps you overcome fatigue and gives you an extra ounce or two of courage when you need to pick up the phone and ask more questions.

Gaining a better understanding of what the employer needs

Sometimes it's the best *informed* interviewee who gets the job. Employers frequently complain about the fact that people who turn up to interview don't seem to know very much about the organisation. It's surprising how little effort it takes to undertake above-average research on target employers. Start to create a research file, including cuttings and print-offs from web pages. Use the **Organisation Fact Sheet** below to collate key facts.

In the past, detailed research meant spending a lot of time in business libraries. Today, the Internet will tell you most things you need, but you need to spend time researching the right things. How long has the organisation been in business? Where is it based? What are its main products, services, and competitors? Then focus on the people involved – who are the key people in the organisation? Who will be interviewing you, and what are their roles?

Make sure your research is up to date. What has the organisation been doing recently? Dip into trade journals or search different product names to find out, but you may learn a great deal by clicking through to the 'press and media' part of an organisation's website and downloading recent press releases. If appropriate, call up the employer and request a recent annual report or similar publications. You can find a great deal of information about the organisation from a range of sources:

- The organisation's website or documentation.
- Media coverage.
- Current employees.
- Former members of staff.
- Suppliers, parent organisations, and partner businesses.
- Other industry or professional contacts.
- Staff on reception on your way into the interview.

Research as if you were investing in the business. Wherever possible, supplement your research through conversations with anyone you know who has worked at this organisation in the past, or contacts who know the employer well (for example, a contractor, consultant, or other kind of supplier).

Getting shortlisted means building relationships

Persuading an organisation to offer you an interview isn't always easy. As Chapter 1 outlined, organisations

Organisation Fact Sheet	
Name of organisation:	
Location:	Main contact:
Telephone:	Email:
Website:	Social media page?
How did I find this role/organisation?	
Nature of business:	Ownership of business:
Number of locations/sites:	Number of years trading:
Key people:	
Main competitors:	Key products/brands:
Any other important information:	
Names and job titles of people conducting interviews:	

are interviewing fewer people face-to-face, and in uncertain times they will tend only to shortlist 'identikit' candidates who have pretty much done the same job before. Even being an obvious fit for the job doesn't guarantee an interview. The main reason is volume of traffic. If a job is advertised, in print or online, it attracts a lot of attention – which is why some recruitment specialists refer to job advertisements as 'candidate magnets'. If you're up against 500-plus other applicants, your chances of getting an interview are slim, even with a brilliant CV. This numbers game is more of a feature than it was 20 years ago. Increasing numbers of jobs stay unadvertised, under the radar (find out more about the hidden job market in *How to Get a Job You Love*).

If a job is advertised, then you will probably have to supply a CV or an application form. Much of the information in this chapter on analysing the job will help. However, people get onto shortlists for all kinds of reasons, and the most common reason is that your name has already come up in conversation. You're a known quantity. That doesn't mean you have to be a networking expert or self-promoter, but reminds you to get as close as you can to possible organisations outside the job application process. This could be about meeting hirers at conferences or other events. It might be undertaking an internship or contract work – even temping increases your visibility and improves your chances of getting interviewed. And don't neglect the simple value of face-to-face meetings. Take every opportunity to meet people in person. While an email or phone call can be forgotten within minutes, face-to-face meetings are remembered. So, when investigating potential jobs, take as many opportunities as you can to visit people in their workplaces.

During the interview process, take any opportunity that comes your way to establish an early relationship. Sometimes when a role is advertised you are given the name of a contact you can ring to ask questions about the job. Do exactly that – asking smart questions impresses far more than trying to press the merits of your application.

You have alternative sources. Talk to anyone you can reach who can tell you something about the organisation. You may already know someone who has worked there recently. Close contacts may be able to introduce you to existing or past staff, contractors or clients. Your question is 'What are they really looking for?' The answer, both in terms of content and the language it's expressed in, is enormously helpful when you're pitching for a job. It will also help enormously during the interview itself.

Zooming in on the job

Use every job-related document you can, supplemented by personal and website research, to make sure you really understand the job. Keep a record of how you came across the job as you may be asked this at interview. Gather information, starting with the obvious. Some of the evidence will already be documented for you in the Job Description – job title, duties, major responsibilities, where the role fits in the organisation. Then look at the Person Specification or Profile – documents describing the ideal candidate in terms of skills, competency, experience, and personality. Against each item on this list start to sketch out matching stories from your past (see Chapter 8 on storytelling as a key interview technique).

Don't be surprised if the Job Description doesn't go into the level of detail you'd find helpful. The document is written for a variety of purposes, not just to inform candidates. If you feel you need to know more, that's a healthy impulse. Successful candidates know that they usually need to go well outside job documents to get under the skin of a role and find out what an employer is really looking for. That process of decoding is vital, and the shortcut is to enlist the help of other people. Talk to anyone you know who has ever worked for the organisation (including interns), interviewed for a similar role, hired for a similar role. Keep asking questions about what the words in the document mean and what evidence will work best to convince people you can do the job. Asking people for this information is much more powerful than just examining websites, because you start to pick up the right terminology – learning not just which of your skills to talk about, but *how* to talk about them.

Breaking the code

The goal here isn't to get special preference or push yourself to the front, but to *decode*. Decoding may seem like an odd idea. After all, most job descriptions are fairly straightforward lists of skills and qualities. Or are they? Experience reveals they're not quite as transparent as they seem. They can be out of date, vague, or downright misleading. Employers often list too many requirements or raise the bar so high that no single candidate could ever fit the bill. Sometimes a job description is a poor compromise between competing views, especially if it's written by a committee. If it's a new job, it may not have been thought through. Talking to people who really know the organisation enables you to get a realistic picture of what the postholder will actually need to do, and what success looks like. (See the 'Top 10 questions' checklist at the end of this chapter for improved job interrogation.)

Start by looking at job documents with a highlighter pen in your hand to pick out key words. Look at the information which is given the highest priority.

Pay special attention to the language used to describe skills, personal qualities, and the outcomes to be achieved by the job. This is the language you will meet in the interview room.

Next, you are going to match yourself against the job. Don't neglect this stage because it seems obvious or hard work – painstaking analysis is the only way you ensure a high rate of question prediction. Take a pad of paper or a notebook. Divide a page into two columns. In the left column, list every element of the employer's shopping list which seems important. Then, alongside, note down your matching evidence. You don't have to write huge amounts – sometimes a single word or short phrase will be enough to remind you of key experiences. When you have completed both columns, you're ready to match information. Firstly, edit your CV so it aligns itself to the role. Often this can be done by introducing one or two extra phrases, or changing the order of bullet points. After that you can write a punchy covering letter – list the top half-dozen areas of your CV which match the most important requirements of the role. Finally, use this breakdown to plan the answers you will give at interview.

You start with an outline picture of the job, but your task is to dig much deeper. Your aim is to work out the *top six items on the employer's shopping list*. Why six? Although Job Descriptions often name a long list of requirements, there is always a weighting towards the things that are deal-clinchers – the elements that matter so much they will always be covered at interview. The place to find these in documentation is where you see phrases like 'key responsibilities' or 'key result areas'. This is the employer's indication of how success will be measured.

Ten steps to improved decoding of job documents

1. Examine everything, carefully, to ensure that your written application and question preparation covers **all the angles**.
2. Look at the **order** and **weighting** of job information. Requirements mentioned first and given most space are your big clues about top value items on the employer's shopping list.
3. Work out **where the job fits** in the organisation structure, ensuring your language matches the seniority of the role.
4. Pick out **skills** required and think about range and level (see Chapter 2 on naming, measuring, and framing your skills).
5. Decide which **achievements** are vital for your CV, and what back-up evidence to retain for interview.
6. Study the **language** used by the organisation in its website and documents, not just about the job but in the way it describes projects, activity, and success.
7. Pick up **key phrases** and use them occasionally in your application and at interview.
8. Spot desired **personality** characteristics and make sure your examples show how your working style matches.
9. **Cross-check** what you learn from research against feedback from contacts who can answer the question 'What are they really looking for?'.
10. Identify and conduct background research on people who are **decision makers** in the selection process.

Interrogating job requirements means that you're easy to process. Bearing in mind that CVs are often read by relatively junior HR staff, if your top ten pieces of evidence match their top ten requirements, you may automatically be heading for the next round.

Interview problems arising from your CV

If you've submitted a CV or application form, you might assume that an interview will be entirely about your work history. Occasionally interviewers will only have skim-read your CV, so you may have to unpack some detail. Some interviewers will make very little reference to it because they want to probe other areas; others will go through it line by line.

To anticipate interview questions arising from your CV, think in terms of plus and minus factors. Where you have presented positives that strongly match the job, an average interviewer may simply get you to talk through them once. Repetition bores listeners so don't use the same phrases you used on paper; tell the stories in fresh terms, and have new material up your sleeve. Positive information may also prompt probing questions: What exactly did you do? What were you, personally, responsible for?

Negative information in a CV is a bigger problem. This might be the wrong information, or the lack of it. It may rule you out, or may lead to some very uncomfortable questions. So look brutally at gaps (see **Q32**) or problems in your CV. If there is something important missing, don't simply hope for the best – include compensating evidence in a covering letter (for example, if you lack specific training, talk about experience which has given you a similar knowledge base). Negatives may also be things you can delete. Ask yourself 'What things in my CV might keep me off the shortlist?' If you've secured an interview, ask yourself 'What things in my CV will this employer be worried about?'

Q19   What do you think of our facility here?

This is an icebreaker which gently probes your knowledge of the organisation, a variation on 'What do you know about us?' (see **Q21**), and therefore a good chance to drop in one piece of information from your research. Mention any previous visits you've made to this site or other locations. Even if the building is in need of a facelift, say something positive. You might pick up on historical features or any aspect that is clearly innovative or well designed. Your comments on what you see should reveal something of your knowledge of the business:

'I love the high-tech feel to the building, and the fact that people smile at you in the corridor!'

Q20   How do you feel about working in this location?

An employer gives quite a lot of attention to the address at the top of your CV, and may worry you'll turn the job down because of its location. A long commute may prove expensive, impractical, or might simply wear you down. A role might require you to move house or live away from home during the week – so your willingness to relocate may be probed. Your main strategies:

- Show enthusiasm for the new location: *'I've always liked this city – I came here a lot when I was a student.'*
- If the location is not the most desirable, even more reason to emphasise the fact that you've thought about it: *'I've worked in different places, and the most important thing has always been the job and the people, not the location.'*

- *'I'm used to a long commute – it gives me valuable thinking time.'*
- *'I have no problem considering relocation, and other options. I'd be happy to talk about the best way of making things work.'*

You don't need to decide about travel or relocation immediately, but show that you're taking the idea seriously and considering options. If you're offered the job, consider enquiring about flexible working (see Chapter 13 on things you might negotiate).

✴Q21   How much do you know about us?

If you are unprepared for this question, you should not be sitting in the job interview (see also **Q6**). You owe it to yourself to learn as much as you can about any organisation offering an interview. For almost any job in the world you can go online and find out a great deal about job content, challenges, learning opportunities, and career prospects. If you know nothing at all about the role, begin with the basics – go to a site such as www.prospects.ac.uk to get an overview of sectors and jobs. Look at the organisation's website, and similar jobs advertised by other organisations. Ask around to find people who can give you an insider perspective.

Spend at least an hour on the Internet researching the organisation – so you can discuss its main products and services, recent developments, headaches the business is facing, or awards it has won. Try to determine how the department you want to join fits into the bigger picture. Find out, using LinkedIn, as well as the organisation's website, something about the people who will be interviewing you. There really is no excuse for turning up and claiming ignorance or saying you haven't had the time to prepare. Provide a concise overview of your findings:

'I understand the business went through a management buyout last year, and since then you've diversified considerably. I believe you're opening two new regional offices this year.'

'Clearly you've been a key player in this sector for a number of years, and you've made a big impact recently with your new product range, so I was pleased to see this role come up. . .'

If this is the first time you have come across this organisation, try not to let that show. If the connection was made through your personal network think whether it's relevant and helpful to mention a name. If you know someone who works at the organisation, it's probably best to declare it now. On the other hand, don't risk falling on your face by pretending you know senior staff better than you do.

Q22 What important trends do you see in our industry?

Doing your homework properly means **researching the industry as well as the job**. This homework will probably involve talking to people rather than just desk research. Prepare yourself to speak knowledgeably about:

- The industry – is it rising or falling? How far is it vulnerable to external factors such as overseas competition or automation?

- What issues are hot in this industry right now? What are people worried or excited about?
- How does this organisation perceive its effectiveness in dealing with these trends and issues?

You should relish this kind of question as a great opportunity to show you have done your research and have valid reasons for wanting to join this organisation.

Go to the **Organisation Fact Sheet** (page 40) to determine if you have enough information to speak intelligently about the industry. Check relevant websites and publications, and keep copies of relevant articles. Pick up the names of key people and organisations. Try to gain a picture of the way this organisation sees its future, and demonstrate that you can be part of it:

'Clearly the biggest trend is the way that conventional newspapers now need to have a live web presence with up-to-date video material. With my journalistic background and my experience of website design, I am really excited about your plans to relaunch your title early next year.'

Q23   What do you identify as our biggest opportunity? What do you feel is our market advantage?

Show you are thoroughly prepared with an in-depth knowledge of the industry, lead products, and key players. Find out how the organisation differentiates itself from the competition. Talk about specific services or products and their respective brand strengths. Begin by talking positively about the organisation, moving into detail:

'Your brand is based on providing high-quality, reliable products. It seems clear that your main competitors

are chasing high-volume, low-margin work while you still have an edge in terms of quality and reputation.'

Q24   What could we be doing better?

This question obviously has its dangers. If you're aware of recent problems the organisation has experienced, it's best not to mention controversial issues or bad publicity. This is a good prompt to make modest suggestions about quick wins (see **Q84**).

A really astute interviewer may ask you to identify weaknesses in the organisation's market position. Make sure you don't criticise individuals or teams. Tone matters here. Are you going to offend someone in the room? Are you going to sound naive or arrogant? If you are up for a senior role you will have made enquiries about an organisation's strengths and its reputation. Conduct an informal SWOT analysis: Strengths, Weaknesses, Opportunities, and Threats. You should be able to say something about all of them. One technique is to focus on a past weakness:

'I think a weakness in the past has been your difficulties going over to wireless technology. However, I see from this week's Financial Times *that you've introduced a completely new product range. . .'*

It's safer to talk about external factors: the economy, currency exchange rates, costs of materials, or the impact of new technology. Then talk about market positioning and ways you might help this organisation to gain an advantage. If you don't want to sound over-confident you can always begin with a question:

'Well, naturally I can only give you an outsider perspective that doesn't take account of the complexities

of the problem, but my reading of your market position is that you are perhaps over-reliant on two or three big customers. Is that comment wide of the mark?'

Q25 There's a lot of jargon in your CV. Can you translate it into plain English?

Technical, 'insider' language can not only be off-putting but can alienate interviewers. A smokescreen of impenetrable language shouts out 'non-transferable skills'. Don't fill your CV with technical terms unless you know it will only be read by people with specialist knowledge. If you do use jargon, be sure your terms are up to date, and anticipate probing questions designed to check your real level of knowledge. Where an interviewer uses jargon for this purpose, you can be comfortable using matching language, but otherwise explain what terms mean in everyday language:

'My apologies – I'm so immersed in the job I sometimes forget that these terms don't have wider currency. In plain language, what this technology does is. . .'

Top 10 questions to ask yourself (and others) when interrogating job documentation

1. What kind of job is this? (This helps you cut through excessive detail and decide what the main purpose of the role is. For example, is it a sales job, a project management job, or is the job about people?)
2. How does the job make sense? (If it's a new role or an adaptation of one or more existing job, it may not have been road-tested.)

3. What abilities matter most to the organisation? (Seeing the difference between 'nice to have' and 'must-have' will give you big clues about which questions are likely to come up.)
4. If the list is extensive, what factors *really* matter? (The job description may list dozens of compe-tencies, for example, but only about 6–8 can be probed in any detail during the average interview.)
5. What level of skill is required? (and what experi-ence would be considered relevant?). Learn to name, frame, and measure your skills (page 24).
6. What do the skills look like in context? (Getting people to describe what gets done in the job helps you to build a picture of what tasks are performed, and how frequently.)
7. What kind of people normally do well in this kind of job? (Find out how long the last postholder was in the role.)
8. Which parts of the list are non-negotiable? (For example, if specific qualifications are named, is there a way around this?)
9. What's most likely to come up at interview?
10. Which half-dozen pieces of your evidence are most likely to secure an interview?

4

Initial impact
MAKING A POSITIVE FIRST IMPRESSION

First glance

With a job interview, most candidates worry about the finishing tape and don't think about the start of the race. It's an urban myth that a conclusive judgement is made in these opening moments – if interviewers could decide that quickly, interviews would be *much* shorter. No one can work out your skill set in these opening seconds, but important views are formed – about your personality, intelligence, and whether you fit. In other words, several boxes are ticked before you've said more than two sentences.

If you sound agitated or cross because of a difficult journey or poor directions, that's your opening message. If you sound bored or irritated by the questions you're asked, you begin by showing indifference or arrogance. If you look and sound pleased to be in the room, you're moving things forward. One early judgement interviewers make is how *personable* you are: Do you make the conversation feel enjoyable? Are you responsive, readily answering questions and volunteering information? Your evidence will be tested shortly, but the right kind of first impression can take you closer to a job offer than you think.

Opening signals

Early assumptions are hard to shake. Most candidates believe they can do nothing about this fact, but of course it's your job to manage that initial moment. In under 20 seconds an interviewer makes judgements based on a range of signals:

- How you **look** (scruffy, over-dressed, professional? Like a visitor, or someone who works there already?)
- Your **emotional state** (flustered, worried, uptight, relaxed?)
- How **easy** you make the conversation (are you personable, friendly, open?)
- How you **speak** (clear, articulate, too quiet, too loud, too fast?)
- Your **confidence** (assured, attentive, nervous, overactive?)

Strategies on arrival

Every conversation you have on site is part of the interview. Reception and security staff may be asked what you were like 'off camera'. Don't wait in silence looking like a black cloud is hanging over your head – talk to people. Conversations reveal information about the organisation but also warm you up for the real thing.

During the day you may meet people from the department where you might be working. Show an informed interest in the work they are doing. Ask intelligent questions – these will show your homework but may also provide better insights into the job. These staff members will also frequently be asked how you came across, and how interested you seem in the job.

Try to be adaptable if things don't go to plan. The interviewer may be late, or may not have had the opportunity to read the papers properly. The person talking to you may sound cold, going straight into job-related questions. Don't be thrown by the interviewer's mood, strategy, or opening questions. This is the script you have to work with – make the most of it. Going with the flow is a good way of acknowledging that you understand what things look like from the organisation's perspective. Being difficult or icy at the beginning of an interview is an almost sure way of wasting everyone's time, including your own.

Why informal chat matters

Small talk oils the wheels. If you want to ask for something difficult, such as a discount, you get a different result beginning the conversation 'How are you today?' rather than 'What's your best price on this?' Every day people achieve extraordinary outcomes simply by engaging others in warm conversation. Practise small talk. Acquire a curiosity about other people's lives, and you'll discover they respond differently.

The opening moments of an interview may sound like chatting. The first question might be 'How was the motorway this morning?' Interviewers don't ask questions like this just to be polite. They know that easy opening questions encourage candidates to calm down and start speaking. Questions of this kind take little brain power to answer, which means you don't have to work too hard (see Chapter 6 on question strategies). Effective small talk helps you switch into active listening, but it's also an early opportunity to show you'd be a great work colleague – the kind of new hire that makes a line manager look good.

Small talk matters for another reason. Talking in a relaxed way about things that don't matter much allows people to begin to trust each other enough to talk about the things that do. The way you interact is seen as an indication of your likely workplace performance. That may seem unfair to candidates who are self-conscious and tongue-tied at interview, but an interview is your showcase, the moment when the decision will be made, so live with the fact: *interviewers anticipate your future self from the way you are in the room.*

What interviewers say when things go well

- The candidate responds openly to the interviewer's handshake, smile, and opening remarks.
- The interviewee seems to find the questions stimulating and interesting.
- The candidate listens and speaks carefully, respecting the interviewer's point of view, and not interrupting.
- The interviewee responds positively to probing questions and affirms when summaries are correct.
- The candidate opens up as the interview progresses.
- Both parties feel that the conversation has been a useful experience.
- The candidate says a warm thank you for the interview.

Focused listening

Under stress, we listen ineffectively. When your attention is caught by something which feels dangerous, your brain shuts down irrelevant channels. Think of a time when you received some really bad news, and then someone talked to you about a trivial matter. How much did you actually hear?

Plan to listen under stress. It may be difficult to hear questions exactly, so you understand the key words – so practise. Attentive listening provides vital clues about what you should say and how much detail to provide. Pre-packaging material means that you are a much more effective listener. You can keep your 'radar' fully switched on during the interview rather than getting caught up in your inner turmoil of wondering what on earth you're going to say next.

Tips to become a better listener

- Use a relaxation technique in the minutes before the interview begins so you focus less on internal chatter and more on what you're being asked.
- Pay attention to your surroundings. Observing where people are in the room, where you will be sitting, and other things that are going on around you also takes the focus off self-talk.
- Listen to the language the interviewer is using. Try to mirror its style (formal/informal, technical/nontechnical, free-ranging, or tightly focused).
- Pay attention to all the words of the question, not just the topic. That way you give the interviewer the right answer, not just a pre-prepared one.
- Respond with empathy when the interviewer mentions a difficulty or problem facing the organisation.
- Don't be afraid of short silences. You are allowed time to think. If you need thinking time, rephrase the question ('So I think what you're asking me is. . .')

- Don't jump in and say the first thing that comes into your head. Pause, so you're sure you understand the question and you know where your answer is going.
- Prepare answers for difficult questions (see Chapter 11).

Be aware of the talking and listening balance in an interview. Oddly, if the interviewer does most of the talking that can lead to positive outcomes. If interviewers talk a lot, they feel good about themselves and may give you credit. However, if you use this strategy, don't neglect to get across your key messages before you leave the room (see **Q114**).

Gradual disclosure

Imagine you've just taken off on a long plane flight. You chat politely with the stranger in the next seat. At first you talk about the queues at the airport, your destination, and the shortage of legroom. Next you say a little about the reason for your journey. You disclose a few things at the outset, then decide whether you want to carry on talking or watch the movie. In low-commitment chatting there is a tacit agreement that you will disclose small amounts of information, and more detail if the relationship builds. If one person discloses and the other does not, the conversation may feel uncomfortable.

An interview uses an adapted version of social rules. It may feel like a pleasant conversation, but it has an agenda and a goal. Although some interviewers like to talk at length about the role and the organisation, the flow of information is largely one way – which is exactly how it should be. The interviewer builds trust to encourage you to disclose increasingly significant information. You may disclose strengths or problems that are not evident from your CV.

The more you can show that disclosure is happening, the better. Occasionally saying *'That's a great question'* or *'I've never thought about it that way before. . .'* reassures the interviewer that the process is working. However, if you over-disclose, you fail to reach your objective, which is to **get enough memorable information across to move to the next stage of the process**. Most candidates say far too much at interview (see Chapter 6). Excessive information can overwhelm the interview, distract the listener from the most important things you have to say, or simply encourage the interviewer to tune out and start thinking about the next question.

One final point about disclosure. Disclosing damaging information (which often simply means being negative about yourself or previous employers) has an impact. We remember bad news for longer than we remember good news. An interviewer will still be thinking about one negative giveaway several minutes later when you are talking about something else. That's why you need two strategies, both outlined in Chapter 6: **Lines of Defence**, and **Safety Zone Responses**.

Q26   How is this role different from your last job?

A seasoned recruiter knows that, for a person to stay in a job, you need to keep on learning (see **Q17**). You need to have a clear reason for moving on to a new role, which means showing how the new job is a better fit. Start with a positive-sounding opening such as '*This role is much more exciting because. . .*' followed by an appropriate reason:

- '*The marketing budget is much bigger.*'
- '*The challenges are greater.*'
- '*It's a chance to get some hands-on experience.*'
- '*Your machines are the best in the business.*'

Q27 Why do you want to leave your current role?

Think about what is going through the interviewer's mind. Are you genuinely on the market, or just testing it? Do you have a clear reason for job change?

Focus on positive reasons for change, and avoid criticism, implied or explicit, about the organisation. Even the best jobs have their ups and downs, so don't give the impression that you are only prepared to take on a job which is 100 per cent perfect. Don't complain about your employer or demonstrate disloyalty – interviewers assume that's how you will behave in the future. A short, upbeat statement will generally get you past this moment, particularly if it is one of the classic reasons for job change:

- '*I've been through the cycle several times and it's time to do something new.*'
- '*I've really enjoyed the job, but I'm looking for a new challenge.*'
- '*I love the job, but I'd like more responsibility and since my boss is fairly new to the role I can't see a management opening coming up for several years.*'
- '*I've learned what I can in the role.*' (Be careful that your message doesn't sound like '*I've learned all there is to know about the job*' – that contains more than a hint of arrogance.)

Alternatively, take the interviewer into more neutral territory:

- **Industry-wide changes:** *'New technology is making the organisation's product obsolete.' 'Manufacturing is going offshore.'*
- **Organisational circumstances:** *'The organisation is restructuring . . . going out of business . . . has been acquired/merged. . .'*
- **Relocation:** *'The organisation is leaving the area.' 'My partner is moving to a new job in this area.'*
- **Uncertainty and risk:** *'We've gone through three reorganisations in two years and I'd be foolish to think that my job isn't at risk, so it seems sensible to move on in my own terms rather than wait to be pushed.'*

Careers author Daniel Porot has a brilliant concept about ensuring that you don't dwell too much on the reasons for leaving a job. My adaptation of his idea is this: **the attraction of the new must sound stronger than the repulsion of the old**. You score more brownie points by having good reasons why you want a new job than by listing all the reasons you'd be happy to leave your current position:

'As with any job there are some problems. However, the major frustration in the role is that my company can't afford to invest in the latest design software – we're publishing materials that look old-fashioned. That's why I'm very excited about the high-quality work you're producing here. . .'

Q28   What *exactly* were you responsible for?

Weaker candidates talk vaguely about 'management responsibility'; stronger candidates give concrete evidence of how many staff they supervised, their responsibility, and their accountability:

'It was my job to make sure that each member of the sales team was hitting their targets, generating new leads, and feeding back the right information to head office.'

Q29 How much did your last job stretch you?

Walk into this question without preparation and you set yourself up to fail. If you weren't stretched by the role, why didn't you do something about it or move on earlier? If you were stretched by it, why are you looking for a new job? This question seeks to discover what makes a job challenging or motivating for you, and get a sense of how long it takes for you to get on top of a role.

'It was a very exciting learning curve, and in hindsight I can see how useful it was to be thrown in at the deep end. I had to learn fast how to respond to demanding clients under time pressure and at the same time keep costs under control.'

Interviewers often want to know how soon you will get on with the job without close supervision:

'When I started the job I knew nothing about financial software packages, but within six months I was familiar enough with the system to take on full responsibility for VAT returns.'

Q30 How did you know you were doing a good job?

This should be a cakewalk of a question, but frequently isn't. It isn't enough to say that you regularly had good appraisals, because an interviewer has no idea what benchmarks were used. You can refer to specific feedback from line managers or customers. Better still, relate your answer to the bigger picture:

'I think my results spoke for themselves ... Within 12 months we became the UK's main provider of external training courses in this field.'

Q31 What was your workload like in your last job?

Don't complain about being overworked – the tempo may be faster in the new role. Don't admit you were bored or underemployed. If the workload was heavy, provide a few brief details. Relate the details to the position you are being interviewed for:

'As in your organisation, everything is dictated by the end of the financial year and by the dates of board meetings. Those were times when we all put in long hours. The rest of the year we took what time we could to keep on top of system improvements.'

★Q32 There appears to be a gap in your CV. What were you doing?

If you meet this question regularly, rewrite your CV and take more care completing application forms. Deal with gaps, and be honest about your employment history. It's a small world and facts usually come to light eventually (or you will get an ulcer worrying about their discovery). Also, providing false information in a job application form may be grounds for dismissal. If your CV seems incomplete, is confusing or puzzles the interviewer, watch out – this kind of question will come up pretty early. Interview time is often wasted querying typical CV problems: CV gaps, qualifications an interviewer can't understand, and job content that is meaningless to an employer in another sector. Make sense of study that isn't clear to an employer (what did you achieve in terms of applied learning?). Don't just rehash phrases from job descriptions in your CV – talk about skills you *used*. If this question is inevitable, make your answer brief and positive, rather than defensive. For example, if the reason was personal:

'I spent some of that year looking after a relative in the last stages of her cancer. It taught me a lot about personal resilience, and the important things in life. . .'

If you had a long job search:

'I was working hard at finding a new role, and also took the time to keep my skills up to date. . .'

If you took time out to see the world:

'I made the decision to take a career break. It was a great experience, required a lot of organisation, and really added to my skills. . .'

Or if you dropped out of an academic course:

'I made the decision not to finish the course as it wasn't giving me what I needed, so I gained work experience in a number of temporary jobs, picking up skills and knowledge along the way. . .'

★Q33   You seem to have done a lot of volunteering. . .

Even in a lively economy people often work on a voluntary basis (see also **Q73**). Sometimes this is about supporting good causes (it's useful to find out what charitable causes your target organisation supports). Frequently people work for free to gain sector experience, or in the hope of being offered a paid role. Even if you've done this a few times, make your work history sound as if you had some kind of a **plan** in mind. An employer is worried by an answer which sounds like '*I couldn't find anything else. . .*'. It's perfectly sensible to undertake unpaid work if it gives you new skills, new exposure, and new contacts. Talk at interview about what you learned so that it doesn't sound as if you were just waiting for a 'proper' job to come up. Avoid saying it was 'just' voluntary work, under-valuing your experience.

Volunteering can help you develop new skills, gain employer feedback, and make a difference. This question is a great way of demonstrating links between skills you acquired outside work and the demands of the job:

'I spend a lot of my time working as a Scout leader. It's great fun, and very demanding. One of the things people often don't realise about Scouting is that you get access to some excellent leadership training. . .'

If you undertook an unpaid internship, watch for the question 'Why did you stay there so long?' In a tough market you sometimes stay in an unpaid role longer than you planned. Role development may provide a credible reason:

'I stayed on because I was given the chance to work with a completely different team and really understand the business. . .'

Q34 Can you work overtime? Evenings? Weekends? Do you have any restrictions on travel?

Your homework should tell you the hours or flexibility required and the overall work culture. In some places it's a black mark if your jacket leaves your chair before 7pm, while elsewhere even senior managers sometimes leave before 5pm and staff occasionally work from home.

Talk about the demands of the job rather than your restrictions. Portray yourself as someone with a strong work ethic, but don't appear so hungry for the job you haven't given any sensible consideration to managing workloads as well as work/life balance. Therefore, don't immediately say 'yes' to such questions, but seek details and information and respond with both a flexible attitude and evidence of past commitment:

'As you can see from my work history, I'm happy to travel if the job requires it. How many nights away from home would you predict in this role?'

'My last job often required me to stay late to get things done, and that was fine as long as there was some option for late starts or home working on other days.'

You may have detailed questions about working conditions, rates of pay for overtime, travel allowances, etc. – but save these questions until you are offered the role.

Q35 I notice you were made redundant from your last job. Has it been a tough job hunt?

This kind of question might get you bogged down in negative territory. An interviewer does not want to hear about how hurt you feel, how badly you were treated, or exactly where you are up to in your dispute over your redundancy payment. In fact, an interviewer isn't that interested in what happened at all, but is concerned about how ready you are to move on.

If you don't make this an issue, it won't become one. Redundancy has become a common experience across most job sectors; some people have been made redundant more than once. Using terms like 'redundant' or 'given a severance package' reinforces the idea that job loss had nothing to do with your work performance *but arose from circumstances outside your control.* All the interviewer needs to hear is that the experience isn't a problem area for you:

'The merger led to a major restructuring and understandably a number of people were laid off. Actually, it's been a good opportunity to explore something different. . .'

You may be asked about your job-hunting experience. Candidates feel vulnerable talking about periods of unemployment, and where they talk about rejection interviewers may see someone who is lacking energy. Employers get worried by individuals who don't get offers – they start to wonder why so many other organisations have said 'no'. Show that you have been actively applying for jobs and making connections. Focus on the job, not your difficulties finding it. Talk about the people and organisations you have met, and talk about voluntary or project work you have done:

'Looking for another job has been a great opportunity to look at other sectors and organisations and to see how my skills adapt to a range of new contexts.'

'I've been keeping my head up in a tough market – I knew it was going to be difficult, but I've got a plan and I'm getting in front of the right people.'

Be aware that *'I've been doing some consultancy work'* is a somewhat overused excuse for people who have been out of a job for some time (see **Q72**).

Ten steps to creating a good first impression

1. Wear smart shoes and clothes, but break them in beforehand so you look and feel at ease.
2. Be very clear of the names and roles of the people who will be conducting the interview.
3. If you have mentioned any interests outside work in your CV, be prepared for an opening question on this topic.
4. Don't ignore small talk – it may be taken as a reflection of your ability to make relationships quickly.
5. Even with social chat, speak clearly, confidently, and not too quickly.
6. Don't let delays or disruptions get in the way of your performance.
7. If you're offered a drink, don't take it if you're trembling. You'll end up wearing it, not drinking it.
8. Be ready to jump in early on with a detailed discussion of any of the big five interview areas: your skills, your achievements, your career ambitions, your knowledge, your working style.
9. Demonstrate the homework you've done. A lack of interest in the employer is a common reason candidates don't get beyond first base.
10. Don't use live interviews as rehearsals – practise with colleagues and friends so you're match ready.

5

Show and tell

MAKING YOUR EVIDENCE MEMORABLE

You might believe your CV sets out everything an employer needs to know. However, a document is just the beginning. For most interviewers a CV provides some answers and a lot of questions. Drawing out and testing detail is what matters.

Review the CV you used to get the interview in the first place, and try to see it through the eyes of a busy recruiter. Where have you undersold your experience? Where is the interviewer going to want more detail? Can you give tangible evidence of achievements? What new information would it be smart to add at interview? Plan how you will bring out the highlights in your CV. In order to do that, you need to make sure it contains the right ingredients.

Cataloguing your experience

You probably have a CV, but you may be unsure if it's working. Two facts about CVs are evident to those who read them all the time. Many CVs convey information which recruiters find routine and not particularly noteworthy of attention (for example, qualifications you studied before the age of 18, your driving licence, and the hackneyed claims you make at the beginning about being motivated and reliable). On the other hand, CVs often leave out important information which is only revealed at interview.

Make sure that your CV gets across your most important facts in advance. In the interview room, add more colour and detail. Get your head around the idea that an interview performance is about **reminding, not announcing** – you will be *reinforcing material already in the interviewer's mind*, not introducing a great mass of new evidence which may confuse the picture. Your qualities and experience should be clear in your application documents, and then reinforced at interview (where, incidentally, it pays to describe past achievements in slightly different language to the words used in your CV).

Even if you already have a CV, start again with an unedited overview of your experience. You will find the **Experience Catalogue** helps (page 72). This unpacks each job you have held, making sure that you pull out relevant information. If you have not yet written a CV, this is a vital building block. Start with the most recent job. In general, you probably only need this level of detail for the last two or three jobs you have held. If a job you held a long time back adds important information, include that as well.

Career highlights

Now we're going to pull out the very best information. Here you are not going to list one job after another as you do on your CV, but dip into any part of your history to pull out interesting projects and other activities which might be worth including in your CV. Don't worry about the sequence, and don't apply too strict

Experience Catalogue	
Employer:	Job title:
Start date:	End date:
Main duties and responsibilities:	Training received and qualifications obtained:
Skills required:	Special knowledge required:
Key result areas/targets/ outcomes:	Key stakeholders/parts of the business/external or internal partners I worked with:
How I adapted/enlarged the role:	
Achievements in the role:	
Innovations introduced:	
Other important information:	
Why do/did I want to move on from this role?	

a filter – anything which has energised you is possible material. Jot down short phrases to remind you of things you will flesh out later. Put the information down in random order as things come to mind – you can fit them into the right place on your CV later and decide which evidence you use. Go back through every part of your work history; look at old diaries and work logs. Don't forget temporary and holiday jobs and work placements. Then try to remember things you did outside work – for example, study, volunteering, personal interests. Keep adding information until you run out of material.

Career Highlights
Use this sheet to record your career high points, in any order.

For example:

- An interesting project
- Something you initiated
- An activity you led
- Somewhere you learned a new skill
- A moment when you excelled
- A personal or work achievement
- A time when you changed something significantly
- A turning point in your career

Career Highlight:	The role I was in:

Keep adding **Career Highlights** to your list as you remember additional material, and then file it somewhere safe. This is the data that you will use to sharpen up your CV, and the raw material that will form the basis of your well-prepared interview questions.

Balancing experience against potential

In a tight market, employers become more conservative, wanting candidates who have the exact mix of skills and experience, preferring those who have done the job before. The problem with this strategy is that organisations appoint people who won't be stretched. Some employers actively seek potential because they want someone who will grow into the job. It often depends who you are talking to in an organisation. HR staff frequently prefer to shortlist candidates who show they have done the job. Line managers are often more influenced by personality and team fit as much as other factors. If your experience isn't a close match, it's your job to demonstrate potential and help the employer feel that risk is being managed.

Tricks of the trade – techniques interviewers will use on you

If someone says 'It won't be an interview – just a chat', be cautious. There's no such thing as a 'chat' in recruitment. No matter how informal, it's an interview. As Chapter 4 indicated, an interview is a conversation which has a structure, a purpose, and one person is very much in control. This can feel confusing because an interview mimics informal conversation (for example, showing an interest in another person), but unlike a casual conversation with friends, this exchange has a clear goal in mind. It's also an interaction that can affect your future – the next job on your CV will probably have a major influence on what you're doing for the next ten years of your life.

We've already seen how an interview is all about disclosure. Much of the time this will work in your favour, but as we have seen, the wrong kind of disclosure can get you into difficulties. Interviewers are trained to get you to open up so that you reveal new information and add colour and depth to existing evidence. You're presenting your actual personality rather than what you have tried to convey on paper. Your answers will also indicate what motivates you and your likely attitude and working style. If you remain defensive and the interviewer feels you are holding back, you're not getting evidence across. Chapter 6 will introduce you to a technique to ensure you stay firmly on safe ground.

Interviewers plan to open you up like a book. They begin by asking you **low-order questions** – ice-breakers to get the conversation flowing, easy questions you don't need to think about – the weather or traffic (or the slightly absurd, 'Did you get here all right?'). This is largely 'social noise', but your responses are being judged, as you discovered in the discussion on first impressions in Chapter 4. Subsequently you'll find that an interviewer's main tool for getting you to talk freely is the **open question**. An open question might begin 'What have you enjoyed about. . .?' Often open questions begin, 'Tell me about. . .'. They encourage you to unpack information and provide relevant detail. Try not to oversupply in response – being given a blank canvas doesn't mean you have to fill it. You'll hear **closed questions** too. Sometimes these are designed to get at facts quickly. Some closed questions ('Did you enjoy that?') don't open candidates up terribly well, but you can always add appropriate detail.

As the interview progresses, the tempo changes and the interviewer will probably throw in tougher questions designed to make you reflect on your experience more deeply (for example, 'What was your biggest challenge in the job?'). These are **high-order questions**, because they require your brain to get into a higher gear. They usually require a little thinking time.

Closed questions . . .	Open questions . . .
May simply check a date or number ('When did you qualify?').	Draw out your relevant experience and achievements.
May check details ('How big was your marketing budget?').	Encourage you to disclose and communicate freely ('What did you enjoy most about that job?').
May be used to check numbers ('How many staff did you supervise?').	Leave you open to answer however you wish ('Tell me about your current role').
Can be used to contain over-talkative candidates ('Just let me check: what profit margin did you actually achieve?').	May be probing ('Why did you leave your last job?').
May limit you to a 'yes' or 'no' answer ('Did you enjoy that job'?).	May dig deeper for content ('Tell me a bit more about how you handled that problem').

Don't be afraid of pausing for a few seconds (but not too long, or the interviewer may jump in with an alternative question, spoiling your opportunity). If you've done the right preparation, you will have most answers ready. Well-trained interviewers listen carefully and then dig underneath what you say with **probing questions**. These throw badly prepared candidates who only have a superficial grasp of their own evidence. Probing checks what you actually did, and the problems you had to overcome. Questions may probe areas you'd rather not talk about – see **Safety Zone Responses** (page 91).

Here are two examples of typical question sequences used in a job interview. Each one begins with a closed question to set the scene. You can see how different question styles are used as information is disclosed by the candidate.

Question sequence 1: teamworking

- **Closed:** *'Have you ever worked in a team?'* A closed question to establish the simple facts with the briefest of replies ('yes', 'no', 'frequently').
- **Open:** *'Tell me what you added to the team.'* Open to persuade you to disclose information about your workplace behaviours.
- **Closed:** *'Have you ever had to work in an unmotivated team?'* A closed question to determine if you have worked in more complicated situations.
- **Open:** *'What happened?'* The interviewer asks you to set the scene.
- **Probing:** *'What did you do to make the team work more effectively?'* The interviewer probes your actions.

- **High-order probing:** *'What else did you try?'* The probe goes deeper. There's no way out except to be very specific about what you actually did, and why.
- **High-order probing:** *'What would you do differently if you faced the same situation again?'* Another level of probing, this time to look at what you learned from the experience.

Question sequence 2: your IT experience

- **Closed:** *'Do you have a PC at home?'*
- **Open:** *'What do you use it for?'*
- **Closed:** *'What image-processing software are you familiar with?'*
- **Open:** *'What is your experience of working with Photoshop?'*
- **Closed:** *'Can you use Lightroom?'*
- **Open:** *'What do you find most challenging about using the latest version?'*
- **Open:** *'Where have you trained and instructed someone else in the use of this package?'*
- **Probing:** *'Which areas of the program are you less familiar with?'*
- **Probing:** *'Talk me through the way you would convert RAW files into JPEGs.'*
- **High-order probing:** *'What's the most complicated thing you've done using Photoshop?'*

The killer pause

A technique that may throw you slightly is where the interviewer waits in silence at the end of your answer. You need to be very clear whether you need to carry on.

Sometimes a pause like this will draw unwary candidates into saying rather too much. An interviewer will always make it clear if you haven't provided enough information. Sometimes a pause occurs simply because the interviewer is digesting what you have just said, or thinking up the next question. If you speak, you're interrupting the flow of the interview. In general, learn to say less and make what you say effective and appropriate.

Q36 How much do you want this job?

(See also **Q52**.) Think about the reasons an employer might ask this challenging question:

■ You seem to lack enthusiasm for the role. Be clear that you're not just looking for any job, but *this* job: *'OK, let me tell you why I would be really excited to get this role. . .'*
■ You may have over-emphasised the richness of your life outside work, giving the impression that you want an undemanding job to fund your private life. So, make your priorities clear: *'I've given you details about my outside interests to show my range of skills, but let me be very clear that my job is the main energiser for me and I always put work deadlines first. . .'*
■ You may have come across as someone lacking motivation. Talk in more animated terms about what you bring to the party: *'I definitely want this job because it would be a really exciting opportunity to put learning into practice. . .'*
■ Employers are often unsure about people who have had a series of interim or temporary roles. Give a clear reason why you're looking for stability: *'I want to be in a permanent position because. . .'*

Q37 What makes you think you could handle a role as demanding as this?

This question is a polite way of saying 'You don't seem to match what we need, so why should we appoint you?' This is an important opportunity to play your best cards. Talk separately about skills and experience:

'It's my understanding that this position requires the following skills . . . Is that correct?'

List the skills briefly and then seek the interviewer's buy-in. Now select and emphasise those that play to your strengths. If the interviewer names an essential skill that you appear not to possess, either set them straight or – if it is a gap for you – ask what aspect of the job requires it. You may cause the interviewer to rethink the job or open the door to the alternative experience you're offering:

'It's true that I do not have experience with this software package, but the one I've been using is so similar I feel confident that I can get up to speed very fast, particularly if I do some learning in my own time.'

Q38 Your experience is all in the public sector. Do you really feel you have what we need?

In recent years many people have migrated from the shrinking public sector. Moving into the private sector isn't easy if you lack the right experience. In addition, the kind of interview questions you face will be very different. Private-sector employers are often looking for a very positive and motivated attitude to work, and a track record of achieving results. Rethink your experience by rewriting your CV in terms of deadlines, goals achieved, and accountability. Look for examples of where you have saved money, exceeded contractual requirements, and times when you have acted like an entrepreneur – creating things that weren't there before and adding new ideas to the job.

Many private-sector employers start with wrong assumptions about the public sector, believing that staff work short hours, seek an easy life, and don't have to meet real targets. The important thing is to convince an employer that you have the right attitude to work, and you enjoy what you do. Using the right kind of language is vital. If your interview answers are full of public sector jargon it reinforces the idea that your experience is different from that of others being interviewed. Do your research carefully to pick up not only job content but job language. Prepare good examples that do exactly that, but reframe what you have done in terms that anyone can understand:

'I can see why you'd assume that my experience is very different, but the culture I was working in changed considerably in recent years. You might be surprised to hear that in my role I was accountable for specific results, and judged on the basis of customer feedback.'

Q39　You have very little work experience. Why should we consider taking you on?

If you are short on work experience and hear this question, revisit your CV. Have you done everything you possibly can to draw out relevant skills and experience? Have you communicated them on the first page? Have you thought about holiday jobs, Saturday jobs, work experience, unpaid work, times when you were 'just helping out'?

Look again at your experience outside work. Sit down with a friend and draw out every scrap of information you can about **skills, knowledge, and work attitude** from the following list:

- School-based work experience – what did you learn?
- Family commitments – organising your Nan's eightieth birthday party.
- Your studies (see **Q13**) – when did you organise yourself or others, communicate something, research something?
- Your hobbies and interests (see **Q33**) – for example, leadership and coaching skills running a junior football team.
- Personal achievements (see **Q71**) – for example, how you motivated yourself to be a better swimmer.
- Influencing others (see **Q44** and **Q45**) – for example, motivating a friend to give up smoking.

Q40 Describe a time when you had to make a decision under pressure

At times you will make quick, good-quality decisions under fire, often in moments when there is little time to reflect, no one to turn to for advice, and you may lack all the facts. Show how you made a decision and stuck to your guns. Don't hint that you assumed powers above your station (*'I told the security team to close the whole building. . .'*). Try to come across as someone who is not afraid to take the risk of making an appropriate decision – and someone who sees the risks of making no decision at all.

'The computers went down in the middle of a senior staff conference. We couldn't get hold of any of the IT

managers. What I decided to do was to ask our contractors to come up with an interim solution just to keep things going until the end of the afternoon, and then to provide a full report to my boss for 8.30am the next day.'

Q41 Tell me about a time when you had to make an unpopular decision

A review of your **Key Turning Points Worksheet** (page 97) may identify a useful example. A good answer will show how you balanced loyalty to co-workers with the needs of the organisation, and the fact that you have real experience of tough situations:

'I had to cut a project that my team were really enthusiastic about. The market just wasn't ready for it. I decided the best thing was to take the decision quickly before any further resources were used, and then I was direct about it – saying how much we'd learned from the experience, even though we weren't taking it to conclusion. The next task was to remotivate the team by providing a new challenge.'

Q42 Where have you had to introduce change?

This relates very closely to **Q43**. Most organisations go through repeated change, which often requires a mix of clear decision-making, sensitive consultation, and an ability to get things done. Try to find out about recent history. If the last postholder upset a lot of people you will need to emphasise your diplomatic skills. If it's an environment where there are turf wars or power struggles you will need to show how you dealt with negativity or opposition.

Talk about a time when you introduced change when there were barriers to success. Show you can consult appropriately and involve key people, but you get things moving:

'I can see that the last thing you want here is someone bulldozing through new ideas without consulting. In my last job I had to relocate our research function, and I realised that there was a range of stakeholders I needed to talk to before putting plans in motion. The most important thing was to make people feel they had been listened to properly. . .'

Q43   How do you consult and inform other staff?

Keeping people informed and feeling 'in the loop' helps oil the wheels. Think about your communication style – do you like to communicate informally, in groups or as you walk around, or perhaps more formally? Do you prefer to communicate verbally or in writing? Whatever your normal style, indicate flexibility in approach, depending on the situation, and show how you do it well:

'Communication was very important in my last position because, to complete our work successfully, we needed to liaise very closely with the client and learn about problems as quickly as they occurred. I saw it as my job then to communicate as quickly as possible to everyone on the line – often that meant walking out onto the floor and talking to team leaders, and making sure the message was passed on within ten minutes.'

Q44   How do you motivate other people?

Prepare examples focused on motivating colleagues or direct reports. Think about varying examples:

- **Improving or maintaining performance** – for example, in sales or customer support roles.
- **Helping people stay motivated in difficult situations** – for example, where others have been laid off.
- **Dealing with underperformers** – without creating resentment or hostility.
- **Managing change** – and persuading people to accept it.

You won't be believed if you say you get it right every time, so have at least one example of a time when it was difficult to motivate someone and you adapted your approach. This might be a good time to talk about energising fellow team members, even if the context is outside work. Describe 'push' leadership skills (driving people towards goals), and 'pull' leadership skills (drawing out the best from people). You might also probe what motivational skills are required in the new job.

'Although people are motivated by very different things, a good place to start is to ask them about their most important goals, and then ask them for an honest view about what gets in the way of results.'

Q45 Tell me about a time you coached someone in the workplace

It's common to be asked questions about developing, coaching, and mentoring other members of staff. Don't get into too much detail (it may be confidential anyway), but briefly describe the situation or problem you were trying to resolve, what style of intervention you used, and what results were achieved. This will demonstrate that you are able to keep two things in focus: organisational objectives, and the needs of the individual you have helped. The best answers show that you are flexible enough to try out multiple strategies:

'I had problems persuading one of the older members of my team to up his game. He kept saying 'you can't teach an old dog new tricks', but I got him to think about the way he could get alongside some of our apprentices to get them to improve their performance, and putting him in this fatherly role did the trick and he changed his own working practices to be a good role model.'

Top 10 interview mistakes that will lose you the job

1. **Crashing at the start of the race**: You can lose the job in the first minute of the interview by not thinking about your initial impact. Sounding flustered, confused, irritated, being too loud, or inaudible – any of these could lose you the job from the outset.
2. **Looking like an outsider**: Leave your coat, umbrella and bag in reception. Just take a slim folder into the interview room containing the documents you need so you will look like an employee rather than a visitor.
3. **Over-delivery**: Candidates often say too much. Interviewers are initially bored if you drone on, but then find something negative in what you say. Saying too much means the interviewer can't cover the full range of questions. Practise compressing

evidence into good short stories no more than three minutes long.

4. **Being too predictable**: If you simply repeat information that's already in your CV, you lose the interviewer's attention. Have new examples ready, and new ways of describing what you've outlined in your CV.

5. **Concealing your skills**: Practise talking about what you're good at, so it sounds convincing, effective, but not big-headed. Describe the problems you faced, what you did, how you did it, and what the result was.

6. **Failing to match evidence**: You only get a chance to pitch a small amount of information about yourself. Everything you offer, whether it's about your education or your hobbies, should relate to key tasks required by the job.

7. **Digging holes**: Prepare for difficult questions probing areas where you feel sensitive, such as unfinished courses, missed targets, gaps in your CV. Plan short, upbeat responses which show you're in control of your career: 'What I learned from that experience was. . .'

8. **Apologising for your work history**: Employers respond well to candidates who present all their learning and work as a single coherent picture. Don't suggest your career is composed of random events – show how your experience makes sense as a continuous story, then talk about how the job is the natural next step. Show that you are not after any job, but perfect for this job.

9. **Making empty-sounding claims**: Weaker candidates say what they thing *should* be done or what they *would* do; stronger candidates talk about what they *have done*, allowing their strengths to

come through. Most candidates use the same clichés – they're highly motivated, self-starters, team
players and will go the extra mile. Don't waste your
breath making empty claims – show, rather than
tell, by giving great examples.

10. **Asking inane questions** such as 'What exactly do
you do here?' Ask questions about how the role
will grow and develop, not queries you could have
answered by spending two minutes on Google.

6

Being brilliant in short bursts

COMMUNICATING THE THINGS THAT MATTER

Information in small packages

How many answers are you likely to give in an interview? Depending on the level of detail, at least 20 and possibly as many as 60. Here's the million-dollar question: How many pieces of information will the interviewer retain? The answer may surprise you. An interviewer may take notes, but by the time she's driving home, it's unlikely she'll remember more than three or four things you've said. With some candidates almost nothing will be remembered.

Strong applicants decide in advance what messages matter, and ensure they get them across in the best way possible. Communication in interviews is about *disclosing information that matters and making sure it sticks*. Too much information, and your key messages are lost in the fog. Too little, and you've failed to score enough ticks on the interviewer's mental checklist.

You will probably decide in advance how you are going to communicate vital messages around a range of topics. For example:

- What makes you a particularly strong candidate for the job?
- Your unique mix of skills and experience.

- Your personal strengths.
- Your attitude, particularly your willingness to learn a job quickly.
- Projects, sectors, or organisations you have worked with.
- Issues which you believe may be worrying the interviewer (see Chapter 8).

Since an interviewer is going to remember only a handful of points about you, make them positive. If the main things remembered about you are that you were recently made redundant, you're feeling a bit low, and you're unsure of your transferable skills, your application is unlikely to go any further. Once you have secured an interview, the most important task is planting the right messages firmly in the mind of the decision maker.

Tips for keeping your answers short and to the point

- *Practise.* Anticipate killer questions by speaking prepared answers out loud two or three times.
- *Don't get too detailed.* Don't recite the full job description for every task.
- *Don't dwell on trivia.* Don't give a ten-minute explanation of your journey when asked 'How was the trip here?'
- *Don't give too much context.* Learn how to set the scene quickly without getting involved in overcomplicated descriptions of organisational structures.
- *Don't hold the floor.* Deliver your answer quickly, clearly, and then hold back to allow the interviewer to engage further with your answer or move on to another question.

Topics you'd rather avoid

When you're preparing for interviews there are probably questions you hope to avoid. These are topics where you know you are vulnerable – more likely to stumble, to blush, and to come up with an inadequate answer. You'll probably say too much, or say something that will plant a negative idea in the interviewer's mind.

When you think about likely questions, some of them make you cringe or want to hide. These questions are likely to make you clam up or allow negative information to leak. **Q27**, **Why do you want to leave your current role?** might be a good example. There are many question topics which press people's buttons. As we have seen, you can predict questions about skills, strengths, weaknesses, past experiences and personal motivation. You're probably more worried about those which probe problem areas. Perhaps you dropped out of a course of study, changed jobs rather too frequently, or spent a long time temping. Perhaps your last job has little obvious connection to the roles you're currently chasing. You might be explaining a gap year or career breaks. Or maybe you don't want to be asked 'Why are you on the market at the moment?'

Staying safe

Prepare yourself for the questions which reflect the doubts and concerns of the interviewer. Don't dig yourself into a hole. In my book *How to Get a Job You Love* you can read about **Safety Zone Responses**. These are short, upbeat answers you have ready prepared for questions like this – the ones that make you tongue-tied or bring you out in a cold sweat. They get you past these small moments of crisis and into safer, positive territory. These responses are brief, upbeat, get you out of difficulty, and at the same time communicate your strengths. Being brief prevents you getting bogged down in difficult details. Being upbeat focuses the listener on the positive (interviewers are good at remembering negatives). The answer moves you on from a difficult past to focus on the future. So, for example, if you were talking about being made redundant, you might say *'Like a lot of people I was laid off when the organisation restructured, but it's given me a chance to focus on what I really want to do. . .'*

Spend more time on these issues than any other, preparing answers of no more than three sentences. These answers should deal with the matter as quickly and positively as possible. This book is full of example Safety Zone Responses (see, for example, **Q14** on qualifications, or **Q27** on the reasons you're job-hunting).

Write down your answers, then try saying them out loud. Say them two or three times until the words feel natural, and then write them down again using the words you've found comfortable. You don't have to learn them word for word, but know the shape of your answers.

Lines of defence

So, think about the areas of questioning which make you feel least comfortable – where you are least sure of your answers. The problem becomes bigger as soon as you react badly to an enquiry. That's why you need short, uncomplicated statements which ensure you move forward, rather than get stuck. Safety Zone Responses deal with the issue, convey one single positive fact, and allow the interviewer to move on to the next topic. However, some tricky topics need two lines of defence. That means having a short, simple answer as your first defence, and a more detailed but equally well-prepared answer as your back-up.

A single-breath summary can sometimes be enough to get you out of the minefield and into safer territory. If you are asked why you were made redundant, don't be defensive or cast your employer in a bad light – far better to nail the problem very quickly (see **Q7** and **Q35**: *'The organisation restructured and several posts were made redundant, which prompted me to think about the kind of work I'd really like to do. This role. . .'*. Most times the interviewer will mentally tick a box and move on, but a seasoned interviewer may push for more information – "Why did you wait for your employer to make you redundant if the job was so unfulfilling?' or 'Talk me through that decision'.

To take an example – if you dropped out of your degree course, offer a short, uncomplicated, positive reason – perhaps *'I decided to get some real world experience.'* That may be enough. If an interviewer wants to know more, have a second line of defence ready: *'I wasn't enjoying the course and I wasn't convinced it was adding to my employability. I decided to look for work and train on the job.'* With some difficult areas you may even have a third line of defence.

Secondary defences will still be brief, but will do one thing very clearly: they will show that you make decisions about your own career, that you actively seek out interesting work and learning experiences, and seek out new challenges. Lines of defence keep your chances alive longer and boost your confidence. Don't get caught in the crossfire without a two-defence strategy. And, in general, give short answers to questions where you're in difficulty, and (slightly) longer answers to topics where you can respond positively.

Achievement stories

Writing your CV, you've probably already come across the fact that employers like to see evidence of achievement. Let's unpack that a bit and think about how it might play at interview. Firstly, think about *why* interviewers want to hear this information. CVs often make great claims, but employers are looking for hard evidence. Most skills discussed at interview can't be tested, so an interviewer needs to question your work history. The 'test', if you like, is being convincing about *what you have actually done*. Stronger candidates don't wait to be pushed and probed – they package their answers so that the evidence is clear.

An equally important reason for talking about achievements is that it's much more interesting to listen to than bare facts. Achievements come embedded in stories, which capture attention and ensure you're remembered. Achievements inform, convince, but also entertain.

You might struggle with the idea of achievements, believing that the things you've done aren't really grand enough to deserve this title. In fact, interviewers don't expect descriptions of earth-shattering events. After all, huge achievements are already specified in your CV. What 'evidence of achievement' really means is convincing, brief, *detail*. What you did with the raw material of an event, problem, or challenge.

Tell stories which show skills in action. Focus on times when you took on a challenge and overcame difficulties, or where you went the extra mile in terms of customer service. Unpack evidence about how you invented a new solution or way of working, or rewrote the rule book. If you were part of a team, concentrate on what you added to the mix – times when projects would have failed if you had not been involved.

Sometimes achievements in your non-working life bring your skills and qualities out best.

Where you can, attach numerical evidence to achievements – sales won, profits gained, costs controlled, the size of budgets controlled, or teams managed. Have these figures at your fingertips, and be prepared to defend or explain them. Make sure your achievements are interesting and punchy, and have a few extra stories up your sleeve ready for a probing interview. Don't just jump straight in with your achievements – build the context up properly – how big was the problem? Don't describe an achievement without showing the size of the challenge you faced.

Decode, translate, and project

In summary, building on your understanding of how to make skills transferable (see Chapter 2), learn how to:

- **Decode** what an organisation is really looking for – what does success look like?
- **Translate** what you can do into language an employer not only understands but finds exciting.
- **Project** yourself authentically, talking about what you're good at without getting in someone's face.

Focus on high-impact events

Start to assemble useful evidence by looking at critical incidents from your past – important moments and turning points, for example:

- A time you faced a major challenge.
- A day when you worked out of your depth.

- A moment when you learned something or adapted your working strategy.
- The beginning or end of a major project.
- A day when you solved a difficult problem.
- A day you made, or damaged, an important relationship.
- A time you received praise or tough criticism.
- A day when you left work on a 'high'.
- A time when your contribution was noticed.
- A day when you feel you made a difference.

Use the **Key Turning Points Worksheet** below to list these highlight events – situations which may have involved risk, but led to concrete results. Trawl your work history for useful examples, and for each one say something about the nature of the problem, the skills you used, and the outcome you achieved. This evidence-gathering process is also very useful when looking at competency interviews (see Chapter 10).

Look in particular for important events in the past two years or so; you will have good recall of detail, they carry more weight as recent events, and are more likely to be probed. However, don't exclude evidence from deeper in your work history, particularly if this allows you to mention important skills. Prepare to talk about projects that went well – but also prepare to discuss activities which failed or weren't entirely successful, but useful learning experiences.

Q46 You've mentioned your sales experience. How good are you at selling?

(See also **Q105**.) Recruiters are often sceptical about CV claims and ask direct questions like this. This question doesn't just seek evidence of where you have sold,

Key Turning Points Worksheet	
Role I was in:	
Event or problem:	
Skills used:	Outcome:
What I learned:	

but where you have sold *against resistance*. Selling a newspaper when you work in a newsagent's takes no effort; selling expensive goods in a shop takes more skill, while gaining a sale from a telephone sales call is rather more demanding.

Trawl your memory for a time when you might have sold something:

- which was a high value item
- which took a long time to get a buyer decision

- which had complicated features
- where the buyer initially said 'not interested'
- where the buyer said 'not now'
- where the buyer said he or she could find something cheaper
- where the sale was achieved through a cold call
- where the sale led to a long-term customer relation-ship.

'I've never formally worked in a sales job, but my job required me to sell ideas to busy journalists. They are difficult to get hold of, don't return your call, say they are too busy and that they're not interested. I learned how to win them over and get them to print the story my client wanted to get out there.'

You may be asked how you deal with objections or customer resistance:

'If a customer is saying no, that's good news because they're talking to me. I need to know what kind of 'no' I'm dealing with – not at this price, not now, not this product. Then I work hard at helping the customer feel that I am there to solve problems, not just to make a sale.'

Sales jobs fit a spectrum between simply looking for business leads, pushier techniques looking for a one-off transaction, and consultative selling where it may take a long time to win a long-term sales relationship. Sometimes consultative selling is highly technical or advisory, where you spend a lot of time helping clients with particular needs:

'My engineering job doesn't look as if it has a sales dimension, but it does. I had to work alongside customers, training staff how to use our equipment. Naturally that

involves discussions about upgrades and support contracts. These clients gave us an extra £1.2 million in business last year.'

Q47   Where have you made cost savings?

Employers are attracted by staff who can either save costs or identify efficiency savings. Fairly exact figures are required:

'I decided to review the full range of contractors who were supplying design services and by cutting down from 22 to 6 providers and managing contracts we achieved a 40 per cent annual cost reduction.'

If your career has not included an obvious contribution to cost reduction, think through past jobs carefully and ask yourself where you spotted and recommended:

- more efficient ways of working which saved time and money
- duplicated orders
- deals or discounts
- equipment or software which saved costs
- cheaper suppliers and resources.

Q48   When have you had true bottom-line accountability?

Senior candidates face this kind of question. If you're arguing that the buck stopped with you, prove it with hard evidence. Were you responsible for both income and expenditure? What controls did you have? What happened if targets weren't met? What did you do to make sure they were?

With high-level roles, for example, heads of function or company directors, you may be asked if you have had 'full P&L responsibility', which in its tightest definition means that you are responsible for income, expenditure, and profit for one area of the business. If you haven't had that level of responsibility, say so honestly, but talk about the level of experience you've attained:

'I had no control over income levels. My responsibility was cost control, and we came in 12 per cent under budget in year one and 18 per cent under budget in year two.'

Q49 Talk me through the way you manage a project

This is a great opportunity to talk about your experience with projects, which might include experience outside work. Use the **Key Turning Points Worksheet** (page 97) to help you identify times you initiated projects yourself, managed one given you by someone else, where you faced obstacles and challenges, and perhaps where you had to change strategy to get things done. It might help to break down your discussion of the project into five simple steps:

- The problem you needed to solve, or original brief.
- How you got your initial project plan signed off, and who you had to influence.
- How you kick-started the project.
- Snags you hit along the way.
- How you reached a successful outcome.

If you've received project management training, mention it, but don't get bogged down in theory. Even if you haven't undertaken training in this area, providing a step-by-step approach shows that you are capable of working with goals in mind, and capable of dealing with each stage of a project's life cycle. This is a great opportunity to make good job content sound great:

'I'm responsible for organising the company sales conference. I start by putting the date in my diary and then working backwards from there to identify all the critical steps, such as booking speakers and confirming travel and accommodation arrangements. Then I look at what needs doing within the next six weeks, and allocate tasks accordingly. The main thing with an event like that is not to let it creep up on you with important things unplanned.'

How do you cope when you have to manage several projects at one time? Don't exaggerate your abilities, or portray yourself as a wage slave who takes an ever-increasing burden of projects. Show you can handle a full workload:

'I have frequently handled overlapping projects in the past, but whenever I take on a new project I always check whether I have the resources and people available to meet the deadline. I know this is a busy place. For me, the key thing is understanding which projects are important as well as urgent, and being clear about what can be sidelined when something unexpected comes along.'

Throw in a bounce-back question if you feel comfortable: *'What opportunities would I have to use these skills here?'* This gets you useful clues about the kinds of projects handled, and organisational expectations about how things are monitored.

★Q50 Where have you had to work under pressure?

Review your worksheets to find strong, recent examples. If pressure is a daily event, mention that fact and talk about non-routine pressure – how you respond in a crisis. This kind of question is often directed at those returning to work after some time out of the market. Arm yourself with examples to reassure the interviewer that you haven't lost touch with workplace pressure:

'I've been concerned not to lose my "edge", so I enjoyed the opportunity to organise a number of big fundraising events for our local hospice. Believe me, organising sponsorship and guest speakers, and selling 300 places is no picnic – especially when you only have 12 weeks from start to finish.'

Be prepared for the kind of interviewer who counters: 'I mean real pressure!' Make sure your example is about genuine pressure, not just another day in the office.

Q51 Tell me how you added value in a role

Key turning points (see page 97) reveal important moments – times when you noticed something going wrong, dealt with a difficult problem, turned something around quickly, made a vital intervention, or took advantage of an opportunity. Find examples where you went beyond your job description:

'Although my job was to manage my boss's diary, I discovered that I was really good at researching and tracking down the right people for him to talk to and setting up appointments with brand new contacts.

That brought us in a lot of new business. No one had done that in my job before.'

Going the extra mile is often about combining a positive attitude with an imaginative approach:

'This summer our biggest client started to make noises about being unhappy with the service we were offering. I went straight round and had a meeting with their buyer. The timing was dead right. Later that afternoon he was having a meeting with our main competitor. I put together a six-point plan for ensuring quality and improved delivery. The buyer thanked me for coming over so promptly and rang me that evening to say we had retained the contract.'

Q52 I'm coming to the conclusion that you don't have the right experience for this job. Do you want to try to change my mind?

This question is more friendly than it sounds. Most of the time an interviewer will not give you any clues that they have written you off, but will either curtail the interview or stop listening to your answers in any detail. Here is a rare example of an interviewer who is giving you a half-time score. Don't react badly. Recognise the person's concerns, and acknowledge that you haven't yet got the right evidence across.

You may not have explained your experience properly. In which case, focus now on the evidence that really matters: *'OK, so I'd like to say a lot more about what I was doing in my last job. . .'* Alternatively, perhaps your experience doesn't yet feel like a match to the job description. If so, get the interviewer to focus on the problems that need to be solved, and then argue the case that your experience, even if unconventional, offers you the skills to deal with the task:

'I realise that the job description talks about sales experience, but I'd like to clarify that my role has been all about building long-term customer relationships which lead to repeat orders. . .'

Don't fail to address any wrong assumptions that the interviewer has made about experience, training, or qualifications:

'I am not certain whether I stressed my experience in designing websites in my spare time using professional software. . .'

In the worst-case scenario, when it's perfectly clear you don't have the experience required, agree with the interviewer – it's your only chance of rescuing victory from the jaws of defeat. Then talk about your potential and why you feel confident you can grow into the role. Employers sometimes buy confidence over experience, and then value the opportunity to shape new staff rather than risk someone who has a fixed way of doing the job.

Q53 Do you feel your career has become stuck?

You may be asked how your career and pay have progressed compared with your peers, perhaps with the implication that you should have moved ahead more rapidly. It helps to know how frequently people switch jobs in your sector. Some fields demand long-term stability, while in others candidates are expected to move on every two to three years. Candidates who enjoy stability may give the impression that they only job hunt when forced to do so, while others show a drive to seek new opportunities. If you have stayed in a role longer than the norm, talk about a valid reason – for example, if the role was subject to change:

'My CV might suggest that I did the same job for 20 years, but in fact the role changed enormously, as did the level of responsibility. . .'

Be especially careful if you spent time earlier in the interview stating how unfulfilling your role has been:

'Although I've been with the same organisation for 16 years I have in fact worked through a variety of roles. I was lucky to be working on projects which always required new learning and offered fresh challenges – until very recently.'

Demonstrate that your career choices have been active rather than passive:

'I've looked at a number of better-paid roles, but I decided that the company I was with offered me far better training opportunities than I could get elsewhere. Now that I am fully qualified, however, I want to achieve the going rate for the job.'

Q54 Would you consider this role on a short-term basis?

In the past, jobs were either permanent or temporary roles. The labour market has changed because of increased flexibility. For workers, this can mean flexi-time or working from home. For employers, this means new ways of filling jobs, including interim and fixed-term roles. What starts out advertised as a permanent role may change part way through the hiring process to something short-term.

If the employer is interested in you but you insist that you're only interested in permanent work, you may talk yourself out of the process. The actual working arrangements are in fact best resolved when an employer decides that they want you. That's the best time to negotiate anything – hours, money, the nature of the contract (see Chapter 13). At this stage of the conversation get the employer to talk about **the problems the job solves**. Ask the same kinds of questions that you would ask if you were an external consultant:

'Ideally I'd like a permanent position, but I'm really interested in working here, so I'm happy to look at alternatives. Why don't we start by looking at what you need? What problems are you dealing with?'

Talking about 'alternatives' makes you flexible, without committing yourself. You have, however, shown a strong interest in the organisation, and started to get to grips with its biggest headaches and greatest opportunities. That way you get a clear idea of what success might look like. Help an employer think through the challenges of the job, and offer yourself as a matched solution. If you manage this conversation well, you may persuade the organisation to make a temporary position permanent. Employers are often far more flexible about this than you think – but only when the need is clear and they have decided that you are the answer to the problem.

Top 10 ways of getting your primary messages across

1. Keep your purpose in mind. What are the three to five main messages you want to get across?
2. If it's a closed question seeking facts or numbers, answer very concisely.
3. Respond with detail, but not too much. The interviewer may be happy with your initial response if it is focused. Saying too much increases the chance of introducing negative ideas and information.
4. Anticipate through your preparation exactly where an interviewer is going to probe. Imagine that each piece of information you put in front of the interviewer is like bait on a fish hook. Which answers are going to make the interviewer bite?
5. Keep it conversational. Do not sound rehearsed, even if it is.
6. Accentuate the positive. Put negative aspects in the best light.
7. Give relevant details. Quantify. (How many people worked for you? What results did you achieve? What costs have you saved?)
8. Do not give monologues. Ideal answers last from 30 seconds to three minutes. Don't feel you need to tell your life story. As in advertising, you don't have to give every detail of a product to gain a sale.
9. Show strong interest in the questions and excitement about the role.
10. Leave on a high note. End the conversation with some great questions about the future of the role and the organisation (see Chapter 12).

7

Fitting in
REVEALING THE RIGHT PERSONALITY
CHARACTERISTICS

It's all about chemistry. . .

Personality traits are not always easy to assess in interviews, but they are an important component of an effective workforce. Well-matched personalities can make great teams, and the right 'chemistry' can provide a congenial work environment. Employers frequently use this term to describe the complex art of shaping good working relationships. An interview can examine personality factors in depth (perhaps assisted by personality testing – see Chapter 9 for more on testing and assessment centres). However, in practice, questions can reflect simplistic thinking ('Are you a team player?') or a misunderstanding of the characteristics required by a role.

Your personality influences the way you communicate, listen, and win people over. It shapes your ability to cope with rejection, criticism, and emotional or time pressure. Some employers seek defined personality characteristics such as extraversion, dominance, flexibility, robustness. How they get at this evidence varies. Untrained interviewers tend to ask direct, ineffective questions such as 'Are you a self-starter?' Experience shows interviewers that candidate statements are largely meaningless; what works best is a detailed investigation of past behaviours. Some employers even say they 'hire for attitude, train for aptitude' – most skills can be taught, but mindset is difficult to shift. Motivation is very much a part of personality (see Chapter 8).

Specific personality traits are essential for many roles. For example, patience, tact and empathy are helpful in a range of people-facing roles. For sales roles, selectors will often look for the ability to build trust and win people over quickly. Leadership roles require an ability to influence others' behaviour and self-awareness of your personal impact. Other roles rely more heavily on your thinking style, your flexibility in changing circumstances, goal orientation, and the ability to think analytically, plan, and manage projects. Some roles require emotional stability – working under pressure and in the face of criticism. You won't match all requirements – we are all a mix, with some factors stronger than others, and there is no 'right' balance. Senior roles are often held by very different people. One company director might be a strong analytical thinker not well attuned to people, while another might shine at building relationships. A charity fundraiser requires good communication and persuasion skills, but there's a big difference between chasing small, one-off contributions, and cultivating relationships with major sponsors.

Interviewers like to believe they work objectively, matching facts about candidates against carefully measured job ingredients. The reality is that many interview decisions are at a gut response level, highly influenced by personality. In the most extreme cases, interviewers select people they like or – worse still – people who are like them. It's understandable; most of us feel happier with people who see the world the way we do. Even skilled interviewers admit that, consciously or unconsciously, they favour people who they feel comfortable with. One effect of such judgements is known as the 'halo' effect, where an interviewer notices one thing they like about a candidate and assumes that the applicant is strong in all respects. The opposite is also true; one off-putting characteristic can make an interviewer dismiss all of your experience.

Clues about the human element

Examine job documents in detail and highlight any personality attributes you can identify. Then think about how far your personality might match. So, for example, if the job seeks someone who is 'innovative', think of good examples. Visualise the work context so you can get a feel for what the postholder will actually need to do, and then think about what personality characteristics would be most useful.

Pay particular attention when a mix of personality attributes is required. For example, a project manager will need to be 'objective', 'analytical', and 'task-focused', but if the job also involves people-influencing skills, then the job description may include words such as 'flexible', 'responsive', and 'consultative'. Decoding using the tips provided in Chapter 3, list those personality aspects you believe the job requires. Against each item on the list, record examples from your experience of when you have demonstrated these qualities, preparing yourself for the questions in this chapter.

Even in the most carefully structured competency-based interview (see Chapter 10) there is still an unspoken question: 'Does this person fit?' When a new person joins a team the chemistry can change very quickly, and a positive or negative person can quickly change the atmosphere in the workplace.

Personality questions are therefore designed to help the interviewer understand:

- How you will fit into an existing team (see **Q88** to **Q91**).
- How you might get along with demanding customers (**Q106**).
- How quickly you can establish relationships of trust (**Q43**, **Q56**, and **Q96**).
- How you make decisions (**Q40** and **Q41**).
- How equipped you are for a management role (**Q94** to **Q97**).
- How you respond to pressure (**Q40** and **Q50**).
- How well you can multitask and deal with conflicting deadlines (**Q49** and **Q87**).
- How quickly you bounce back from failure or disappointment (**Q58**).
- If you have leadership qualities (**Q99**).
- If you can manage change (**Q42**).

Watch out for topics which scrutinise personality evidence: initiating and managing projects, innovation, teamworking, managing teams, motivating others, responding to criticism, working against deadlines, difficult colleagues or customers, or working with people from backgrounds very different to your own.

Seeing yourself as others see you

Emotional intelligence enables you to observe your own behaviours and understand their impact on others, and so get better at predicting their responses. Interactions can be instinctive, and some are better at handling people than others. You can learn compensating behaviours, but it's always a good idea to listen to feedback about your working style – particularly how it modifies under pressure.

An interview allows you to reveal how your personality plays out at work. Are you comfortable in your own skin? How do you motivate others? Can you empathise with customers, clients, supervisors, fellow workers? Can you see another's point of view? When things get tough, boring, hectic, or chaotic at work, how do you react? How do you help others to manage their feelings?

Depending on the interviewer's agenda, questions on personality can quickly screen candidates in or out. Traits can be viewed either as positive or as negative. Take, for example, the adjectives 'creative' and 'aggressive'. Creativity in an advertising manager is a laudable trait; 'creative' bookkeeping could cause problems. Aggressiveness in sales managers pushing into new markets could be vital to a start-up company, but aggression is something a childcare agency wishes to avoid.

Skilled interviewers are used to candidates who provide examples seen through rose-tinted glasses – when everything went perfectly. You will be asked about times when things went wrong. Talk about projects where things didn't work out as you expected. With practice you can even discuss failures, showing what you learned from the experience. A bit of humility helps, too – interviewers are naturally suspicious of candidates who get everything right. You're not presenting fiction; you're trying to convey what you are like when you are working at your best.

Show you can hit the deck running

Employers want to get value out of staff and get a return on the cost of recruitment. You'll have some time to get to know the ropes, but the chances are that you'll also need to prove yourself fairly quickly. Questions will probe your past to find how long it normally takes you to get up to speed with new projects. What kind of training and support are you going to need to deliver results? With more senior candidates, impact is vitally important. You will need to give tangible evidence of where you have solved employer problems in the past, through your own skills and know-how, but also through consultation with stakeholders and alliances with providers. If you are after top-level responsibility, you will need to provide matching high-level experience and accountability.

'Soft' skills

Chapter 6 looked at achievement evidence. It's fairly easy to list achievements involving numbers, but harder to provide achievement evidence for soft skills, which are closely linked to your working style and personality. Soft skills might include: being diplomatic, winning people around to your point of view, persuading colleagues to cooperate, coaching a colleague, reassuring an important customer. It's hard to put monetary value against these outcomes, but they may be probed most closely and therefore need achievement stories. Think about a time when you had to persuade colleagues to do something they were reluctant to do, or tell someone bad news, or negotiate something from a weak position. Use a simple story structure – what was the problem, how did you act, and what was the result?

If you can't use numbers, talk about other kinds of outcome, such as a happy customer.

✳Q55   How would you describe your personality?

Think first of all about the two kinds of answer an interviewer doesn't want to hear: (1) a long list of over-blown adjectives, or (2) 'I'm not sure'.

Use the list below to kick-start your thinking. Tick the ones that apply to you. What words can you add? Scrutinise language in job documents describing atti-tude and working style. Then go beyond documents – talk to people. Ask friends, family and colleagues what

---

Words that capture my personality

Outgoing	Relaxed
Flexible	Deadline-driven
Innovator	Focused
Listener	Questioning
Good at detail	Analytical
Diplomatic	Empathetic
Task driven	Assertive
Completer-finisher	Loyal
Motivating	Efficient
Spontaneous	Planner
Self-motivated	Leader
High energy	Risk-taker
Imaginative	Analytical

words they would use to describe your work personality. Then find someone who understands your target employer (past and current employees, consultants, suppliers). Your goal is not just to understand job requirements, but to get a sense of what a top performer looks like.

'From what I can see you need a combination of an analytical thinker and someone who is good at handling client enquiries. That's the way I was described in my last appraisal.'

You may be asked about one particular personality trait – for example, 'Do you prefer to work alone?' Be clear about what the job requires. If the balance is completely wrong for you (for example, you don't want to be left on your own, or you hate working in an open-plan office), then maybe the job isn't for you. That's something for you to decide later. For now, try to work out what balance of group working versus isolation the job offers, and be prepared to give examples of where you have worked effectively in both situations.

'I've done jobs where I have worked alone out in the field and others where I have enjoyed having people around me most of the time. It all depends on the best way of completing the task.'

Q56 What kind of people do you like to work with? What kind of people do you least prefer to work with?

This may seem to be about your dream team, but in fact is fishing for past relationship difficulties. Stack up examples about team members, staff who have reported to you, previous managers, and customers or clients you have worked with. Talk about people who have inspired you, energised you. Talk about people you have learned from. If you worked in a good team, say so, and explain why the team worked. This is a very good opportunity to praise past colleagues, which sends out a signal that you work well with others and can learn from a variety of contexts.

Spend more time talking about the people you like to work with, and give a brief answer on the second part of the question. You might just allow yourself one short anecdote about someone who displayed work practices that would irritate the saintliest worker – for example, colleagues who sit on vital information, or people who are sloppy about vital details. Talk about the behaviour, not the person, and be prepared for the follow-up question: 'So what did you do about it?'.

'I like being around people who look as if they enjoy their work and think about how they can do things better. I'm afraid that I am rather less energised with people who don't seem to care what they do as long as they can leave by five o'clock.'

Q57 How would colleagues describe your working style?

Behind this question lies a concern: How self-aware are you? Do you make claims about your working style that others would find difficult to recognise? An interviewer has no easy way of double-checking your picture of yourself against the views of others (although this might come out in a reference). This question shows clearly that claims you make in your CV will not be taken at face value. Inform your answer with evidence, rather than guesswork or false modesty:

'Colleagues tell me I'm good at getting things organised and a natural project manager, and not afraid of ruffling feathers to meet targets.'

'My last boss said she valued having me around because I am open to new ideas, innovative, a good listener, and someone who gets things done.'

Q58 How resilient are you?

Any number of words can, of course, replace the word 'resilient' (other top favourites include *assertive, inventive, proactive, decisive, influential, dynamic. . .*). However, resilience – the ability to bounce back after setbacks – is important in many roles.

'In my line of work you hear "no" far more times than you hear "yes". You just have to keep at it until you get a result.'

Think of good examples which demonstrate how you applied this quality. The best answers on personality show by telling a story:

'My last job required tremendous resilience. For example, the project to develop the new transmission was sent back to the drawing board five times, sometimes for technical reasons, usually because of changes of policy. That got some people down, but I just got on with the job and gave the project the same attention I gave it the first time it crossed my desk.'

'We worked three months preparing a 500-page tender document. On the day the contract was due to be

signed the client announced a policy decision which blocked funding. I called the team together and gave them a pep talk to remind them how much we had learned, and we used the information we had gathered to win several other pieces of work.'

Q59 How determined are you?

Determination is a quality often sought by employers – the ability to stick with a task, overcome obstacles, and keep going until the goal is reached. Determination in one person may of course be seen as stubbornness or inflexibility in another. Dogged persistence can be seen as a negative characteristic in the workplace – for example, where you insist on continuing a failing project because it was your idea.

Easy tasks don't require determination. Talk about times you experienced opposition, complexity, or time pressures. Perhaps you faced personal criticism or objections, or people undermined what you were doing. This is all good evidence of your ability to keep pushing, despite setbacks – times when you stuck to your guns in the face of difficulties and took something to a successful conclusion without causing a staff walkout. Ideally your answer will be taken from a work context, but here's an example taken from a career break:

'I had to be pretty determined to arrange my career break in New Zealand, because I wanted to get an internship with a wine producer, and I was told that competition for places was high, even for locals. Nevertheless, I pulled in favours and rang a few people directly. I got one offer which was then withdrawn because of timing issues, but I got on the

phone right away and told them that I really wanted to work with them, and they let me go on the dates I had planned.'

Your story may well bring out useful competencies (see Chapter 10) such as problem-solving, improvising under pressure, and assertiveness.

★Q60 Tell me about your strengths

It's almost impossible to get through a job interview without answering this common question. What makes you an unusually suitable applicant for the job? Strong candidates resist the temptation to unload empty adjectives: *self-starter, great communicator, team player, natural leader.* An interviewer has heard them all before – from this year's school leavers and graduates. So coming out with that kind of list is really saying *'I haven't bothered to think about this question'* and *'I have nothing to offer that you can't get from someone younger and cheaper'* – both great ways of talking yourself into the reject pile.

Smart candidates start with the organisation's top three to five needs, and then provide matching evidence. It pays to use words that are slightly different from the terms used in the job description, otherwise your answer sounds a little too glib. Then move into a short burst of evidence that reveals where you have demonstrated the abilities you claim:

'I'd like to talk about the strengths that are relevant to this job. My understanding is that you're looking for someone who has top-level influencing skills, good public sector contacts, and an in-depth knowledge of procurement. In my last job. . .'

Don't forget that the broad term 'strengths' allows you to talk about any factors which make you a strong candidate. If the interviewer wants to bring you back to personality factors, look again at **Q55**. The best strengths are usually combinations of personality, knowledge, and skills:

'I think I am unusual – I have actuarial training, experience of technical roles in the banking sector, but also the communication skills to inform and persuade.'

★Q61 And what about your weaknesses?

If you're asked about strengths, a question about weaknesses usually follows. Don't go anywhere near an interview without thinking about this topic. Interviewers pay close attention in the hope that you will say something revealing. Some candidates risk saying *'I don't have any weaknesses'*, but a good interviewer won't let you get away with that – you will be pressed to name at least one, and doing so without preparation is a dangerous game. Practise short, convincing responses about strengths *and* weaknesses by writing them down, then speaking them out loud two or three times, and then testing them out on a good friend. Anything else is leaving far too much to chance, as we are now in the 'make or break' zone of the interview.

Naturally, you shouldn't be as open about weaknesses as you are about strengths. Interviewers will usually admit that they give far more weighting to negative information and remember it much more clearly than all the positive things you have said. So do not, under any circumstances, volunteer information about past relationship problems, culture clashes at work, or poor work performance.

Avoid cheesy one-liners. Some interview coaches say it's acceptable to talk about an 'allowable weakness' (for example, being frustrated by under-motivated colleagues). With confidence, you might try:

'Because service is such an important hallmark of our approach to internal as well as external customers, I sometimes spend a little more time than I should making sure that people get the help they need.'

However, it's safer to discuss one area of personal development you're working on, as long as the problem you're addressing is relatively minor:

'I recognise that sometimes when I am working to tight deadlines I don't always communicate progress to my team as often as I should. I'm working on that with a mentor right now and trying out some new strategies.'

One approach is to turn the question on its head and provide clear and simple reassurance:

'I've looked at the strengths you need for this job and I'm confident I can deliver what you need. If there's anything else I need to cover, that's OK – I'm a fast learner.'

Q62 If I spoke to your former boss, how would she describe your strengths and weaknesses?

Clearly you won't be believed if you say *'My boss would say that she isn't aware of any weaknesses.'* This, is, however, a good opportunity to describe a very solid working relationship that included honest feedback and mutual appreciation of different working styles:

'In my first appraisal my boss told me I was a perfectionist and that could slow things down because I wanted to complete every project perfectly. So I watched the way she worked, and learned to see when it was appropriate to do a "good enough" job. My next appraisal said I was a person who got things done and kept customers happy, which worked much better for both of us.'

Or, where you are on more equal terms with your manager:

'This used to be a kind of running gag between myself and my boss. She would tell me that my strength was that I would get on with the job, but then she'd keep checking in on me to make sure I was making progress. We developed a good system in the end: she'd pretend to leave me alone, and I'd pretend to give weekly progress reports. It worked really well!'

Q63 Where have you operated outside your comfort zone?

This question is exploring your flexibility and how easily you are able to adapt when events surprise you. You should find that the **Key Turning Points** worksheet (page 97) delivers examples of where you've had to respond quickly to new circumstances.

'I had to stand in for our Communications Officer at short notice and deal with an enquiry from a local radio station about a former employee who had been taken into police custody. It was a scary moment, but

fortunately I had been briefed about what I could say verbally before we issued a press statement.'

Q64   What rattles your cage?

Variations on this question are 'What irritates you?', or 'What makes you angry?' This is another tightrope question. Revealing times when you blew your top at work suggests you can't keep a cool head. On the other hand, if you say that nothing aggravates you, you can sound passive. Focus on those areas where frustration is a boost to work performance:

'I rarely get angry, but I can get frustrated when suppliers let us down badly. The trick is to do what you can to solve the problem and then go back to ensure there is a good system in place to make sure it doesn't happen again.'

If you're going for a role which demands passionate intensity (for example, a role campaigning for animal or human rights), then a potential employer would probably be surprised if you didn't talk about strongly held beliefs or a sense of injustice.

Under pressure some personality traits reveal themselves – when things start to go wrong you may become more irritable or less focused on details. Even so, a recruitment interview is not the time to bare your soul. Everyone behaves imperfectly when the heat is on. What you need to do is to convey the impression that you are reasonably robust, expect work pressure from time to time, and know how you will react:

'Pressure comes with the job. I work hard and then play hard to let off steam, rather than letting my work performance suffer.'

'Under pressure I tend to get very focused on the real issues at hand and try not to get distracted when everyone else is running around like headless chickens.'

'Oh, I'm famous at work for pacing the floor like a lunatic on launch days, but that keeps me and everyone around me on the ball. . .'

Top 10 tips for dealing with personality questions

1. Prepare for classic questions on strengths and weaknesses.
2. Think about the way you normally behave and influence others.
3. Dig deep into the job documentation to get a feel for the personality style that would best match the role.
4. Ask trusted colleagues for honest feedback on the strengths and weaknesses of your working style.
5. Practise talking about yourself. It feels odd at first, but you soon get used to it.
6. Don't contradict what you say with the way you act. Your 'non-verbal' messages should match the person you are describing.
7. Do not let your guard down for questions you may think are 'soft' or 'informal'. Everything is part of the interview.
8. Write down and rehearse crisp, upbeat responses – don't memorise them word for word, but have a pretty clear idea about what you are going to say.

9. Make the interview a good experience for everyone else in the room. That shows more than anything you say how easy you will be to work with.
10. Form a 'success team' of two or three trusted friends to meet periodically to discuss career strategies and help pick you up if you experience rejection.

8

Communicating motivation

EMPLOYERS BUY INTO ENERGISED STORIES

What kind of work feels worth getting up for on a Monday morning? We are motivated by different things at different stages of life. Younger workers often seek change and opportunity, while older workers may prefer security. Some seek the potential to earn a high salary; others seek work which feels meaningful. Some live to work, while others are motivated by activities outside the nine-to-five. An organisation is going to invest time and money recruiting you, so wants to know what motivates you – and what keeps you energised in the long run.

In 2013, a famous survey of 142 countries by Gallup reported that, worldwide, only 13 per cent of employees – one in eight workers – feel engaged and committed at work: 63 per cent were 'not engaged' – meaning they lacked motivation and were unlikely to put in extra effort not required by their job description.

You might think about what employers look for in new staff. Yes, they want skills, experience, and sometimes underpinning knowledge and the ability to think. Employers list leadership potential, teamworking, flexibility, and decision-making amongst their most wanted items. The Association for Graduate Recruiters (AGR) reported in 2015 that employers 'are looking for a combination of skills, knowledge and attitude'. That last word is significant. Employers say they're looking for drive, initiative, and enthusiasm, but always add that they want something extra – a positive approach, a 'can do' mindset. *Attitude.*

How do employers identify this characteristic? They face a problem. Almost every CV falls into the trap of piling on endless adjectives. Every job-hunter (no matter what age they are) claims to be a *highly motivated dynamic team player* – or offers similar clichés. Some know how to pep up a CV with high-energy language, but only a few can do this authentically – communicating energy on paper is not as easy as it looks.

An interviewer has only two angles when testing your claims about being a motivated worker – the past and the present. Let's begin with the present. The most obvious source of information to an interviewer is what's going on right now in the room. Do you appear to be an energised, motivated, enthusiastic person? A decision about your energy levels and whether you're a likable, cooperative person is made very early on in the process (see Chapter 4).

You might look and sound like a motivated person, but a skilled interviewer will probe to find out whether this is how you are on a normal day in work. It's all very well to state that you have skills and personal qualities, but you need to back this up. *Evidence* is what matters (see **Q82**). Your past will be revealed in your CV and perhaps also when references are taken, but an interviewer relies most on the material you unpack at interview. Don't forget that this can start with preliminary conversations – for example, in a telephone screening interview, or a conversation with a recruitment consultant.

Top five Motivation Focus Points in an interview

Focus point 1 – building a warm relationship from the outset

An interview is like an audition or screen test – interviewers come to a conclusion about your working style in the first few seconds, even before formal questioning begins, while you're settling into the room. Making the conversation easy forms a strong first impression – about whether you will fit into the organisation. Part of that is about looking and sounding as if you're an engaged worker. Respond positively to questions. When you tell stories, ensure that they're energised.

Remember that when someone hires you their decision is very much in the spotlight on your first day at work – interviewers want to look good by finding new hires who clearly fit in.

Focus point 2 – communicating top skills

Your CV may contain over a hundred facts, but in an interview you will make only a few points. When you discuss your work experience, don't just talk about obvious tasks: show how you added to roles, where you went the extra mile and were stretched. Use every example of a skill to show *how* you used that skill – with commitment, imagination, determination.

Focus point 3 – preparing the right stories

Make sure your story makes sense so an employer understands the shape of your career. Show that your skills are not only relevant, but at the right level. (See Chapter 2 on how to show how well you exercise your skills.)

Tell energised stories to reveal both experience and motivation. People remember stories far longer than they remember information, and high-energy stories even longer. Practice helps – so you leave an interviewer in no doubt that you bring something special to the role.

Focus point 4 – match energy between yourself and the role

Job descriptions give some clues about personality traits, but you can dig deeper. Talk to people who know the organisation well – not to get special treatment, but to decode the attitudes and behaviours demonstrated by the most valued members of staff.

Don't just talk about the best aspects of your personality – *reveal* them through well-packaged examples of where you have performed well. Above-average candidates *show* rather than tell – they communicate stories which show how they have worked with energy in past roles, where they have added value, delighted a customer, or provided new ideas.

Focus point 5 – stay credible and authentic

Effective rehearsal means your answers feel authentic and not as if they come out of a textbook. Rehearsing word-perfect, set piece answers doesn't work – it focuses on what you want to say rather than what the interviewer needs to hear. If answers come out stilted and pre-packaged it suggests this is what you're saying to every employer – and probably means that you're not listening to questions properly.

Be really clear about the stories you will tell at interview, and keep them brief. Match these stories to the role. List what you believe to be the top ten employer requirements on a sheet of paper, and against each point make a note of a skill story. Focus again – don't oversupply information. Summarise the problem you faced, the skill and how you used it, the end result (and maybe also what you learned from the experience). Having these short, punchy skill summaries available in the back of your mind means that you can focus on really listening, and on maintaining a good relationship with your interviewers.

Anticipating objections

An interviewer may start with doubts in mind, and more may be raised by what you say. If you've matched yourself systematically against the role (see Chapter 3), you should be aware of points where your evidence is weak or lacking. You could hope that the interviewer won't notice or won't mention the point. This is dangerous – if an interviewer has a suspicion or assumption and you don't deal with it, it's still there. If you listen to interview panels they often talk about the concerns which candidates failed to address adequately – *even if no relevant questions were asked.* There's only one safe way to nail a concern – raise it yourself. If you suspect that the interviewer is worried about any aspect of your CV, think about tackling the issue head-on:

> *'I expect you're thinking. . .'*

> *'I imagine you might be concerned that. . .'*

Energy and storytelling

Think about a conversation you've had recently which has stuck in your memory. The chances are that it included a good story. We are naturally attracted to stories as a way of interpreting the world. Stories are entertaining, colourful, sometimes funny or dramatic. Human beings love stories.

Remember that fact when it comes to communicating what you do well. Take team leadership skills, for example. You could simply claim that you're good at leading teams. This doesn't go very far, and can irritate an interviewer hungry for hard evidence. You could give the details of what you did in your last role, and improve that evidence by talking about what you achieved. In teamworking, achievement might have come from working with a difficult team member, or where a team was confused about its objectives, or unproductive. This is fairly effective, but how interesting is it to listen to what is effectively a rehash of your CV?

Trying to remember good examples during an interview is hard work, because you have to apply several filters at once ('Will this sound interesting/relevant/impressive . . .?' 'Will it come out right?' 'Can I remember enough detail to answer supplementary questions?'). Having this information ready in the front of your head means you can give more attention to using your interview radar, working out the real agenda.

What works, therefore, is **storytelling** – turning basic facts into interesting narrative. A good story engages the listener's attention. If it's a story you listen to rather than one you read, it will be short, will grab your attention immediately, and will have a memorable ending.

From fact to story

Type of evidence	Example statement
Bare fact	*'My job required information retrieval.'*
Unqualified claim	*'I am good at organising. . .'*
Claim with limited evidence	*'In my last role I had to organise. . .'*
Claim backed up with evidence of achievement	*'Recently I reorganised our risk management records. . .'*
Claim backed up with evidence of achievement	*'As a result, we had 26 per cent fewer legal claims. . .'*
Claim and evidence wrapped into an energised story	*'Let me tell you about how I reorganised things in my department and got some great results without treading on too many toes. . .'*

Using mini-narratives has great advantages. First of all, it's easier for you to remember at interview and far less risky than improvising. Second, improvised, unplanned rambling bores the interviewer and you will unwittingly include negative information. Third, a well-constructed story is easier to listen to: *people remember stories far longer than they remember facts.*

★Q65   What's your career plan?

Are you passive or active in the way you plan your career? Do you have long-term goals? Do you set sail towards a destination, or bob around like a cork in water? Do you have a clear idea for the next stage of your career? Share some of your thinking, but not your wildest ideas, and not your regrets about unfulfilled potential. If your heart is clearly somewhere else, you'll talk your way out of the interview – this job mustn't seem like second best. Alternatively, if you don't seem to have a plan, you're effectively saying any job will do. Remember: **the job you are being interviewed for, right now, should seem like the most important job in the world**. Rehearse a **Safety Zone Response** (see page 91) for this point, demonstrating clarity and flexibility:

'In my career in sales I have worked in both new business development and managing existing accounts. I enjoy both challenges – winning new clients and keeping existing ones.'

Or talk about paths you have considered but not taken:

'I strongly considered moving back into a finance role, but having looked at a number of roles I'm more convinced than ever that I want to stay in an operations role, because I really enjoy being at the sharp end and influencing what gets done.'

There are two exceptions where you can afford to be rather broader in your statements:

- Where you are talking to a recruitment consultancy that has a range of roles that might fit you. In this case try a line such as: *'I'm very flexible as long as I can work for an exciting organisation that's going places, in a role where I have some control over results.'*

- Where you are applying for an entry level position in an organisation with a wide range of roles – for example, a graduate programme. In this case what matters most is that you understand the organisation, its culture, and have two or three simultaneous and realistic plans for how you might build on the opportunity: *'I'm really looking forward to a chance to experience HR, L&D and possibly also purchasing, as I know I am going to want to specialise in one of these areas.'*

A key planning stage when thinking about this question is to listen to feedback from agency recruiters, who often have a finely tuned sense of typical career routes. If you believe that your CV indicates confusing changes of direction, plan an answer which tackles that head-on:

'I'm aware that I could have moved up the ladder quicker if I'd hopped around organisations, but I really enjoyed the organisational culture and I had a series of exciting roles offered to me.'

If you're looking to make a career change, have a clear explanation:

'I've really enjoyed working in human resources, and I've had the chance to do a lot of fascinating jobs. However, I've come to realise that I actually enjoy making a direct contribution to the bottom line of a business, which is why I am now actively seeking a business management role.'

You may be asked about your long-term goals (see also **Q67**). It's fairly safe to assume that the interviewer wants you to talk about a work context, but if you have other goals (fitness, sporting, personal achievement, or learning) and they don't detract from your working commitment, mention them too. If your long-term plan is to run your own business, that is something to keep to yourself.

Q66 You appear to have moved around a bit. . .

Don't be surprised by this question if your work history could be described as 'chequered' (recruiter shorthand for 'never settled down'). Find someone to talk this issue through with, well before you sit in front of a decision maker. The first principle is that you don't offer your CV apologetically (*'All I did was temporary work'*) or throw in caveats such as *'This may not make sense to you . . . my CV's a bit of a jumble sale.'*

Although you may have done many jobs, you only have one career. Get across a clear, unified story:

'I have enjoyed a real variety of work experience, but in every part of my career the thing I have enjoyed most is customer interaction. My experience in hospitality, the finance sector, and retail environments has shown me what first-class customer service looks like. My goal now is to build on that career by finding a long-term position in a sector where I can influence how that is delivered.'

★Q67 Where do you hope to be in five years' time?

This is one of those off-the-shelf interview questions that has never fallen out of fashion. It is not a bad question because it gives a clear time frame. It seeks evidence of drive and ambition, but also checks out how well you understand the role and the organisation. Weaker candidates tend to use a gimmicky textbook answer like the outrageous *'In your job!'*, the very off-putting *'Running my own business'*, or a vague answer like *'I don't mind, as long as I have job satisfaction.'* Be realistic – but also optimistic:

'I'd hope to still be with this organisation, in a position of increased responsibility where I will be able to continue my professional growth while making an ongoing contribution to the organisation's success.'

If the role is one which has a regular turnover and people typically move on after a year or two, a realistic take on the situation may help:

'I recognise with a sales role that you hit a point where things can feel routine, but I've always got past that point in previous roles by seeking new methods of business development or by coaching and managing other staff. Either direction would work for me.'

If asked about how quickly you would like to be promoted, be diplomatic:

'I need to concentrate on the position I am being considered for at this time. That will be more than enough to occupy my attention for quite a while.'

Another tried and tested approach is to adjust the timeline:

'In the current climate, very few of us know what the world will look like in five years' time, so let me tell you what I think I can achieve in the first three months of the job. . .'

A variant on this question is: 'Would you like to have my job?' – as a test of your ambition, or a signal that you're a little threatening to the interviewer. It's usually safe to say something which balances caution with a willingness to get on with the job:

'With all the challenges in the job, I will certainly be kept busy for quite a while before I start to think about my next step in the organisation.'

Q68 Tell me about the best job you've ever had

This is the kind of question career coaches ask – to spot peak moments (see the **Career Highlights** exercise on page 73 and **Q69**). Like **Q70** it helps identify the specific ingredients you're looking for in a job. However, if your answer is going to be credible your 'best' job should have strong connections to the role you're chasing. What you are essentially doing is offering a 'recipe' for job success that should be fairly close to the position on offer. If you were highly motivated by a job that sounds very unlike the one on offer, make as many useful connections as you can, and reinforce the message that the job on offer is what you're looking for:

'That's easy – I loved my job in the recording studio. But that's the kind of low-pay, high-excitement job you do when you're 23. Looking back on it though I can see that it gave me great experience and the ability to get results out of very difficult people!'

Q69 Tell me about a high point in your career

(See also **Q71** on achievements.) If you talk in glowing terms about a job you held in the past, the interviewer may feel that the rest of your career has been a disappointment. On the other hand, if you can't identify a high point, that communicates a lack of engagement. Try linking past and future:

'I think the role I most enjoyed was working as an account executive in a PR company. However, as enjoyable as the job was, it didn't really give me an opportunity to work with top decision makers. This role, however. . .'

Otherwise, seize this opportunity to outline your skill set and its relevance:

'I got a real buzz out of managing the repairs department – ensuring that repairs were done properly, work went out on time, and we kept customers informed and happy. When the business folded I realised that these were the skills I wanted to use in a new role. . .'

Q70   What kind of work gives you a buzz?

Interviewers pay attention when they see candidates who are clearly animated by the work they've done. This happens when they see positive body language and hear energy in your voice. Verbal energy, more than anything, conveys what will really motivate you in a job. Equally, nothing talks you out of a job faster than tired, dull responses that sound as if everything in life is slightly too much trouble. Prepare high-energy stories which capture roles which have motivated you in the past. If your style is naturally quiet and down-beat, rehearse replies that have more uplift. One strategy that helps is to make sure you use phrases such as *'I really enjoyed. . .'* or *'I really get excited when. . .'*

'I always get a kick out of working with committed people and finishing a project on time. For example. . .'

'The thing that floats my boat is being given a problem that everyone says can't be solved.'

'A real high point for me was designing our last exhibition stand. I wanted to do something really different, really high-tech – and it worked!'

Q71 What are you really proud of?

(See also **Q69**.) If possible, provide an answer focused on work. Offer concrete examples: when you won an award or were specifically rated against others (for example, sales turnover, savings, efficiency). You might also think about instances where you were singled out to teach new employees or serve on a special team. Remember that **average candidates make general claims; strong candidates list achievements**. Achievements don't need to be extraordinary – see the checklist at the end of this chapter. Look again at your **Experience Catalogue** (page 72) for suitable examples.

'Just this month I organised a thorough review of our research expenditure. I looked at what we were spending and what we really needed. I was able to rationalise things so we have only three suppliers and we've negotiated an overall 45 per cent reduction in costs.'

Learn how to communicate achievements as short, upbeat stories – people respond well if you do so. You might start with the headlines only:

'OK, I can talk about our expansion into Ireland, designing our new online catalogue, or developing my team. Where would you like me to start?'

Accomplishments outside work are also useful; the restoration of a house, completing a degree, or planning an overseas expedition would all qualify.

'I'm proud of raising £50,000 of funds for a local heritage project.'

'I completed the London marathon under four hours.'

Q72   You've been working recently as a freelancer. Why would you want a permanent job?

Some jobseekers enter into consultancy assignments while looking for a permanent role. A rule of thumb among executive recruiters is that one or two consultancy assignments are experiments; more represent a career decision. Employers wonder whether your career has moved in a new direction – are you really interested in a salaried job? Are you looking for a job because your consultancy business has failed? Will you be setting up in business again once the economy picks up?

'I've been talking to a number of organisations and a company I know well asked me to sort out its logistical problems, which seemed a good idea to sharpen up my skills and knowledge. However, I'm not interested in long-term consultancy work, and I am looking for the kind of role on offer here. . .'

Or, if you have been consulting for some time:

'I made the decision to do 18 months' consultancy work to broaden my sector knowledge and get under the skin of a wide range of businesses. The long-term plan was always to move back into a permanent role,

because I recognise that you have more influence and more chance of achieving long-term results inside an organisation.'

Staff are sometimes retained by previous organisations after redundancy. Again, this suggests that you may not be free to take on new work, and hints that you're building up a consultancy career and not really interested in a permanent role. When an ex-employee is invited back in this way, this shows you're a trusted colleague with high-value knowledge; something your answer can emphasise:

'The offer came as a bit of a surprise to me because I was ready to move on, but I was made a very good offer to provide my services on a fixed-term basis. I did, however, make it clear from the outset that I could only do a maximum of three days a week because I need time to extend my network into new areas of work. I have a very clear understanding that if I find a new role I can tie things up quickly and move on. . .'

Your CV may identify your own consultancy as your current employer. If you make the interviewer aware of your business by listing your website or handing over a business card, you're effectively saying *'I'm no longer interested in working in a fixed role inside one organisation.'* Employers are often wary of people who are directors of their own personal companies as this implies that you have taken a firm step away from salaried work.

'Working for myself was right for that phase in my career and gave me exposure to a wide range of interesting organisations, but I'm very clear now that

I want to spend the next stage of my career working inside a big organisation.'

Q73   Would you consider working initially on an unpaid basis?

Some roles, particularly internships, are unpaid. Consider whether volunteering will add something useful to your CV, and enhance your value to future employers. One danger of working for nothing is that employers only give you low-level tasks and may leave you unsupervised. With more senior appointments the risk is that employers may place less value on your advice because they haven't paid for it. Also keep in mind that, while you are in work, it may be harder to find time for an active job search.

All work is a deal, whether it's paid or unpaid. You may feel the deal is entirely one-sided – your labour given free of charge, but an employer has to provide your workspace and supervision. Seek a healthy trade-off between your labour and non-financial benefits. Work out what they might be in advance and negotiate the ones that matter most to you. Always seek something in return – your contribution will be valued more.

Benefits you should think about negotiating if working as a volunteer:

- You may receive travel expenses, particularly if you are asked to work in a variety of locations.
- You should receive on-the-job training. Throw yourself at a variety of tasks, and keep a learning record.

- Negotiate opportunities to develop your skills, even if this is just for part of the working week where you are attached to a different team.
- Ask in advance for regular feedback on your performance, and a reference at the end of the assignment.
- Seek opportunities to meet new people inside and outside the organisation. Your natural curiosity may prove to be a door opener.
- If a paid post is created, you're a known quantity with a distinct advantage over external candidates.

If you want the job but you can't afford to work for nothing, don't be offended by the suggestion. Continue to show strong interest in the organisation. You might indicate that this mode of working isn't right for you at the moment, but you'd like to be considered for any paid roles that come up in the future:

'I would jump at the chance to work here, but unfortunately my financial situation means that I would be distracted by any other paid job offers that came along.'

Focusing on the employer's needs may unlock the coffers:

'That's a tempting offer because I really believe in what you're doing here. However, I'd like to think that you'd get more out of me if I was firmly committed here by receiving a salary, and if you have a moment or two I'd like to explain why I'd be a good investment. . .'

If you take the offer, see also **Q33** on how you will talk about voluntary work in a future interview.

Evidence that makes interviewers worry

There are many things that might give an interviewer cause for concern, but here are some of the classic danger areas:

What you *appear* to be saying	What an interviewer is thinking
I've changed jobs frequently.	Flits about. Can't stick to a job. See **Q27**, **Q66**, and **Q76**.
My jobs have little in common.	Chequered history and no clear career story. See **Q65**.
My main qualification has nothing to do with my career path.	What do this candidate's studies contribute to the job? See **Q13** and **Q14**.
I have lots of qualifications but little work experience.	Could be a perpetual student. See **Q15**.
I have lots of consuming interests outside work.	Might take too much time off work. See **Q4**.
I am in a secure, well-paid job.	Will probably turn the job down if it's offered. See **Q116**.
I've done a lot of volunteering.	Unable to secure paid work. See **Q33**.
I love taking career breaks.	Will be off again soon – leaving us in the lurch. See **Q32**.
The high point of my career was ten years ago.	Little motivation to succeed. See **Q68**.

Work has been stressful recently.	Looking for a quiet life. See **Q50**.
All my work has been in the public sector.	Won't be able to adjust to the cut and thrust of business. See **Q38**.
I am happy to do any kind of work.	Is this person motivated by any part of the job? See **Q54** and **Q75**.
I believe I have management potential.	No evidence, and probably has a naive view of the demands of a managerial role. **Q96**.
I have been running my own business.	Only wants salaried work until the economy improves. See **Q72**.
I am not sure what I am looking for in my next job.	Unfocused on the right next step. See **Q53** and **Q74**.

9 Tricky interview structures and methods

GETTING PAST NON-STANDARD INTERVIEWS

Telephone interviews

Employers increasingly use telephone interviews for screening during an early part of the recruitment process. These interviews tend to ask a handful of key questions in order to filter most candidates out, and successful candidates will then usually go to a face-to-face interview. It's a low-cost option for checking candidates against basic criteria. Don't be disappointed if the interviewer seems to take little interest and doesn't want to get a bigger picture – the function of this kind of interview is to screen you in or out, so there's little point trying to throw in extra information.

Phone interviews seem low-key, so jobseekers sometimes take their eye off the ball. They require the same degree of preparation as face-to-face discussions. It's much harder to build a warm, working relationship in a telephone discussion. Technology and distance get in the way, and the process can easily feel very cold and technical. You won't be visible (unless it's by video – see below), so you can't rely on your appearance or body language to help with communication. You must rely on your voice to do most of the work – so vary the volume, pace, and pitch. Make sure that you sound interested and enthusiastic. Answer clearly, which might mean slightly more slowly than normal, and briefly – it's even easier for an interviewer's attention to drift, especially as they will have to conduct many interviews at this stage. At the end, ask if there is anything you can add, and throw in one or two questions of your own. (See the checklist on **telephone interviews** at the end of this chapter).

Recruitment consultancy interviews

Recruitment agencies interview candidates by telephone and in person. Sometimes the aim is shortlisting for a particular role. At other times these are registration interviews, getting a broad sense of your experience and skills to match you against a wide range of future positions.

An external recruiter acts as a gatekeeper, deciding whether to put you forward to an employer. A recruitment consultancy makes money by charging the employer if they fill the role, so it is important that you show that you will put in a credible interview performance. Dress and present yourself as if it was the final interview, and treat the consultant as the *eyes and ears of the employer*.

Video interviews

Video interviews continue to grow in popularity as the technology becomes cheaper and more efficient each year. Skype, or a similar software package, is the usual choice. The expectation is that you will be on-screen, so find a computer with a video camera installed or attached. Sometimes video interviews using set questions are recorded. Managers can then see each candidate answering the same questions, and can compare responses.

Employers use Skype interviews to screen candidates quickly, often with little time spent on small talk. A video or Skype interview makes it easier for you to strike up a relationship because you can see each other, but even so, body language and gestures are less easy to interpret on screen.

Dress as smartly as you would for a meeting, but check out how you appear on camera. Also consider what's around and behind you that will appear in shot. Declutter and make the space seem as calm and business-like as possible. Have in front of you the same information you would take into an interview.

Set up a camera on your computer so you can record yourself giving practice answers. You'll start to see what the interviewer sees. The first thing you will notice is that you appear to be looking down, rather than straight at the viewer. That's because you're looking at the centre of your screen. Get used to looking at the camera instead – this imitates eye contact with the interviewer. You may also notice a time lag between sound and picture, and audio is not always as clear as it could be. You can't do much about this apart from speaking more clearly and slowly than you would do normally. Your PC microphone picks up noise in the room, so don't move about or shuffle papers. Under no circumstances should you check your phone or try to deal with some other task on your desk while you are being observed.

Informal interviews – 'it's just a chat'

Never be misled by that word 'informal'. It's always an interview, whether it's on the phone, meeting in a railway station for coffee, or in a hotel lobby. The word 'informal' signals that you're expected to be relaxed and to show how well you'd fit in. Nevertheless, even if it's a 20-minute chat over coffee you are still being assessed against the requirements of the job – be prepared.

If you are invited to meet over lunch, especially if it's for a second interview, this is a fairly clear indication that the employer wants to know what kind of person you are. A relaxed setting can encourage you to drop your guard, but also presents a good opportunity to find out about the organisation and role. If you're eating during an interview, even if it's just a sandwich, don't choose food which you will end up wearing. Turn down alcohol – it disinhibits and blunts your attention.

Competency interviews

Assessment centres and other structured methods will often include competency (or behavioural) interviews. These are so important they get their own chapter, coming up next.

Panel interviews

Panel interviews are widely used, particularly by public sector organisations and charities. They naturally feel more intimidating than a one-to-one conversation. It's undoubtedly harder to build rapport with several people at once, and you may feel interrogated from multiple directions. Panel interviews are often more formal with less opportunity for small talk, making candidates more nervous and stiffer in their responses.

Find out as much as you can about panel members, their function in the organisation, and why the role matters to them. One panel member may come to meet you – use that opportunity to build a relationship. In the room, be clear about faces and names, and note the names of interviewers not previously mentioned. Use interviewer names occasionally as you answer. Work out who the main decision maker is and give that person due attention, but address everyone directly and vary where you make eye contact. If a panel member asks few or no questions, don't ignore them. Panels sometimes include people who rarely conduct interviews, so you may have to be cooperative if you hear awkwardly worded questions. Occasionally panels ask difficult questions without giving you the chance to warm up. If so, take a moment to compose your thoughts – well-structured answers matter here more than anywhere else.

The background theory behind panels is that the more people interviewing, the more objective the result. However, many believe they favour candidates who shine at panel interviews, not necessarily those who will perform best in the job. Panels are often constrained to work to scripted questions, with fewer follow-up, probing questions. If a panel probes your answers, welcome the opportunity to add detail to your evidence. If your answers aren't probed at all, work differently – your first answer may be taken as final. If so, make sure your response covers all the requirements of the question, providing concrete evidence if a competency is being discussed. You might also add 'Does that cover what you need, or would it be helpful if I provided some more detail?'

Panel members usually have a short gap between interviews to compare notes, so make sure you end on a positive note. Ask good questions at the end (see Chapter 12), and say goodbye to each member by name, shaking each person's hand and thanking them for their time.

Seven steps to mastering presentations

Some interviews, especially those involving interview panels, will ask you to make a short presentation. Here are some tips that will help dispel your nerves and meet expectations.

1 Think screen test, not lecture

Candidates often believe the process is about communicating information, but employers want to see you in action, on your feet. Your audience is comparing your performance with the real role. As you stand up, they're thinking 'Can I see this person working in my team?' or 'Would I feel confident putting this person in front of colleagues?' (or clients, or senior staff, or any other likely future audience). Verbal communication skills are being observed, but so are confidence, clarity, and the ability to convince an audience.

2 Meet the task

Normally you will be told how long you will be expected to speak for. Sometimes you'll be given a topic in advance; sometimes you will only be given this 30 minutes or so beforehand. The employer should also clearly inform you whether you are expected to use PowerPoint, and when your slides should be submitted.

3 Focus on the beginning and end

Interviewers are more likely to remember opening and closing words than anything else you say, so it's a good idea to plan and rehearse the *exact* words you will use to start and end – and how you will link sections.

4   Connect yourself to the role
A presentation reveals your understanding of the job. Show you've done your homework and analysed what the organisation is trying to achieve. Reveal connections between this role and your background, and make practical recommendations where appropriate.

5   Practise energy
Don't underestimate the importance of being entertaining – which isn't about telling jokes, but *concise enthusiasm*. Audiences enjoy listening to people who know their stuff and speak with energy about the things that matter to them. PowerPoint, used well, maintains audience attention. Three or four bullet points per slide – plus one image – works well.

6   Observe time limits with great care
Think carefully what you're expected to deliver. Most candidates try to fit in too much. You will probably spend two to three minutes on each PowerPoint slide, so don't expect to get through more than about four slides in a 10-minute presentation – you will probably be stopped at the time limit, cutting out your closing points and denting your confidence.

7   Use PowerPoint only as a support tool
Average presenters apologise for missing slides or for not having enough time, get lost in written notes rather than directly addressing the interviewers, or run out of time. Don't overcomplicate or over-deliver. Avoid handouts until the end as they distract. A few good points made well, with illustrations, stick in the memory far longer than something long and complex. The worst PowerPoint presentations contain too much text which the presenter then reads off the screen. Less is much, much more.

Handling second interviews

In recent years both candidates and agencies have been reporting that employers are taking longer to make selection decisions. They often call candidates back for a second interview. Sometimes this is a scheduled part of the process.

A first interview is generally to establish whether you have the skills and knowledge to do the job. Second (or third, or fourth. . .) interviews are for other reasons. If the first interview confirms you have the right skills, subsequent interviews check organisational fit – an important 'chemistry check' to match you against existing team members. You might have an initial interview with HR to look at your general competencies, and another with a line manager who has job-specific questions. Sometimes you'll be called back to meet prospective colleagues, or senior staff who will want to meet you before the appointment decision is finalised.

Much of the question preparation advice in this book of course applies if it's not the first interview. Follow-up interviews usually probe your experience, your achievements, and your weak points in far more depth. However, their main function is often to find out whether your personality is a good organisational 'fit'. Therefore, you will face questions about working under pressure, resilience, communication style, not treading on the boss's toes, and how you will quickly make an impact. Chapter 7 will assist here.

If you are invited to a second interview, review the topics that came up in the first meeting. Think about the responses you gave. Were there any questions you didn't answer so well? Were there any topics not covered at all? Notes may have been taken. Assuming they were, which of your answers will be picked up and probed? However, don't be surprised if the second interviewer has limited information about what you said in the previous meeting. Sometimes a second interview will explicitly probe answers you gave in the first, discussing areas of concern, but this happens less often than you'd expect. Be prepared to repeat your evidence and make sure your Safety Zone Responses are ready.

Ask, diplomatically, about the reason for each selection event. Ask who will be interviewing you, and how you should prepare. Raise your game at a second interview; don't put in a repeat performance. Think about answers where you didn't completely address the question, and rehearse new examples. However, don't assume continuity. Interviewers sometimes pass notes on, but you may be asked the same questions again – answer them as thoroughly as before.

Tests

You might be asked to take one or more tests. Some roles require skill tests (for example, measuring typing speed). Intelligence tests cover verbal, non-verbal, and numerical reasoning. Personality questionnaires have no right or wrong answers, but are designed to give clues about the way you respond in a range of situations. Here, the best strategy is to answer honestly rather than trying to second-guess what the recruiter is looking for or trying to impress. If you have undergone personality tests in the past, you may want to talk about past results – for example: *'No problem, but interestingly tests pigeonhole me as an introvert, when in fact I am pretty good at establishing new relationships quickly.'*

Take a note of the names of tests the employer will be using. Go online to research them and to try practice questions. Ask the employer what feedback you will be given after the testing process – you may find the results very helpful, especially if the process involves a structured interview.

Assessment centres

An 'assessment centre' is a fancy term for an event which includes a variety of selection methods. Assessment activities can include tests (see above), goal-setting and other team activities, and in-tray exercises. They usually mean working with specialist assessors, and at least one interview, sometimes competency-based (see Chapter 10), sometimes focused on test or exercise results. Assessment events can be demanding experiences, but also an opportunity to receive useful feedback. Sometimes these events are competitive; at other times they recruit against standard criteria so no one, or everyone, may be selected.

Read joining instructions extremely carefully; don't be afraid to ask for further information if anything is unclear. An assessment centre is a complicated event, and very few people understand exactly what they have to do. Use the Internet to find out more about the tests and events you will experience – many providers offer online test samples and other materials such as in-tray and group exercises. Rely as much on your personal research as the information you're sent by the employer.

When you get there, pay close attention to group tasks and discussions as these often indicate leadership potential, decision-making, and teamworking style. In discussions, don't dominate conversations but ensure you seek other people's opinions and include everyone in the discussion. Do make clear suggestions and be decisive if the task requires it.

Be aware of the most frequent reasons people do badly at assessment centres. One is poor preparation through inadequate attention to briefing materials, another is allowing their overall performance to be knocked back by difficulties experienced on one task. Others are routine interview flaws writ large – lack of research on the organisation or sector, superficial awareness of challenges being faced, a poor understanding of what is required in the role, and a failure to anticipate questions.

Q74   What would be your ideal job?

This might puzzle you. Why does the interviewer want to know about your *ideal* job? Surely it's *this* job that matters? Interviewers know that employees are more motivated in roles which match their preferences. You may have reflected on your best job ever, and developed a sense of what 10 out of 10 looks like in your job wish list (if you haven't, read *How to Get a Job You Love*). This is probably not material you share with an interviewer – the danger is that you describe something much better than the job on offer. Talk about a solid overlap between your ideal role and the job available:

'I am looking for a company that really wants to offer added value to customers, and a role in that organisation where I can make a real difference to staff attitudes and behaviours.'

Q75   What parts of this job appeal to you most?

If you can't talk about why you might enjoy the job you're unlikely to be offered it. Fall back on the preparation you've done, matching the needs of the employer against your personal career aspirations. Focus on two or three elements that really matter to the organisation:

- *'I love the fact that the job is really focused on client relationships.'*
- *'I particularly like the problem-solving elements of the position.'*
- *'The team that I would work with looks terrific.'*

If the question turns to those aspects of the job which are less attractive, show a healthy realism:

'Of course every job has its less fulfilling aspects, and although no one enjoys writing up weekly reports you and I know it comes with the territory.'

'You're operating on a split site which I guess is a problem for everyone. . .'

Leave the interviewer in no doubt about two essentials:

- Any drawbacks are of minor importance.
- You very much want the job as it stands, and you don't have an unrealistic or idealised picture of the role.

Q76　If you take this job, how long would you expect to stay in it?

(See also **Q27**.) Even in difficult times some employers report difficulties finding talent. In addition, if someone leaves shortly after being hired, the time and cost is painful for an organisation. An initial strategy is to point to your track record to date:

'I have never been a job hopper. I'd like to be in a role with a long-term future.'

Try to get a sense of how long people typically stay in the organisation. If you are meeting with a highly entrepreneurial company, you do not want to say something along the lines of *'I am looking for a place to stay until I retire.'* However, if the company suffers staff turnover problems it might be appropriate to say, *'I'm happy to commit myself here for as long as you want me.'*

A secondary question in the interviewer's mind is 'How long before we get some return on the time and costs of hiring this candidate?' So, rather than predicting timescales for moving on, talk about performance:

'I'd like to hope I'd still be in the organisation in a few years' time working on interesting projects, but I recognise that I've got to prove myself initially, so I'd like to talk about what you hope to achieve by the end of this year. . .'

Q77 Don't you think you would be better suited to a different type of organisation?

Often the interviewer will add something extra to this question – for example, suggesting you might be looking for a bigger organisation, or one which is more up to date or traditional. Listen carefully to what is being suggested, and avoid going on the defensive. Try to work out what you said (or neglected to say) to plant this idea. Try a quick probe:

'Could you perhaps give me a sense of why you've come to that conclusion?'

This question could of course be a buying signal. You've indicated the right skills for the job; the interviewer is just concerned that you may be uncomfortable working in this particular organisation. Will you be disappointed and move on quickly? Your answer should show how much thought you have already given to this question, and how this organisation is exactly right for you just now:

'Good question. I feel now's the time to move into a small company environment where I can gain experience of a number of different functions and be involved in the overall strategy of the business.'

Q78 Why would someone with your experience want to work *here*?

If this question is asked without cynicism, it's a straightforward opportunity for you to match your skills and qualities with the needs of the job. However, an unprofessional interviewer might say something that appears to be critical or subversive. Don't be drawn into any kind of negative comment. If the question really is loaded and you find yourself listening to a disgruntled employee's monologue running the organisation down, listen and keep your distance. You may be getting useful insider information which will help you decide whether you want to take things further.

This is a good moment to show how this job is the natural next stage in your career journey:

'So far all my experience has been in the public sector, but in every job what I've enjoyed most is reorganising systems and finding efficiency savings. I believe this skill set will gain far more recognition here.'

If the interviewer is singing the praises of your present employer, again use this opportunity to give a valid reason why you want to move here:

'Yes, I've always worked in large organisations, but the reason I'd like to move into a small business is that it's all hands to the pump – you get to do what's needed, not just what's in your job description.'

Q79   When has your work been criticised? How did you respond?

This probing question offers the interviewer an opportunity to consider:

- Your tolerance for criticism, and ability to learn from mistakes and accept feedback.
- Workplace relationships.
- How easy you are to supervise.
- Your openness to learning and doing things differently.
- Your ability to bounce back after setbacks.

Suggesting that your work has never been criticised carries no credibility, so plan a couple of examples where you received helpful feedback and changed your approach. This is also a broad strategy for talking about weaknesses (see **Q61**). Refer to your **Experience Catalogue** (page 72) and **Key Turning Points Worksheet** (page 97) to refresh your memory.

'I was taken to task by my last boss for communicating too often by email – and he was right. It's much better to walk over to someone's desk and maintain a proper relationship. Also, you are more likely to get cooperation and hear an honest answer about potential snags.'

'*We were under pressure to get our new payroll software up and running. In a project meeting the technical people would not commit to an implementation deadline. Since they wouldn't, I did. After the meeting they complained to my boss saying I took a decision above my pay grade. This was in fact a sensible decision, but I learned to negotiate things more carefully and be clear whether I needed authorisation before setting targets.*'

Don't choose a scenario where you really made a major error of judgement – you'll dig a hole you'll never climb out of. Select a situation in which, even though initially you were overruled, sooner or later your thinking prevailed. The only thing left is not to hammer the point home at the expense of your adversaries. Try to show win–win. If you didn't win, it was no big deal for you and it is best to convey the impression that you did not take it personally.

You may decide to talk about 'grey area' situations where your judgement was not completely right or wrong and appropriate risk had to be taken:

'*Last year, in the big snowstorms, only a handful of people got into work. I thought we should say thank you, especially as many of them were worried about getting home, so I decided that the team should have a free lunch that day. Next day the MD felt the decision was overgenerous and set a precedent. It was no big deal, and I accepted her decision.*'

Q80   In what ways has your career prepared you to take on greater responsibility?

You should have an idea about how your experience to date provides the right foundation for a more demanding role. Give examples to show where you've acted in a more senior capacity:

'When my immediate supervisor was called away for jury service, it was even longer than anticipated – he was tied up for several weeks. During his absence I was responsible for running the division and I enjoyed it immensely. Deadlines and production adhered to schedule, and I was also able to make some recommendations about improved performance when he returned to work, which were well received.'

'When I started preparing designs they needed to be double-checked by my line manager, but in the last six months I've been allowed to send them straight out to clients. I feel I am on top of the job enough now to supervise other designers.'

✷Q81 Everyone on the shortlist has similar background and experience. Why should we give you the job?

It's likely that everyone who shortlisted will be able to do the job. You've got an interview to find out what puts you ahead of the competition: *Why you?*

Weaker candidates reach for the adjective box, claiming they are more motivated, team-minded, commercial, committed. That works to a certain extent, because employers buy into attitude as much as they buy into facts. But the best way of conveying the right work attitude is through hard evidence.

This is a good opportunity for a brief recap. Talk about two or three strengths that are vital to the role, and speak about how you use your skills and knowledge. Suggest that you have a mix of skills and knowledge which others may not possess. Reinforce the idea that you really want to be part of the organisation, and you have a concise and powerful answer:

'Not only do I have the technical understanding of the software itself, but I have the communication skills to show staff and customers how to get the best out of it. I think you'll find someone with my technical skills fairly easily, but you might find it harder to get someone who is capable of translating complex information into everyday language – and retaining customers on the way.'

Q82 Your CV makes a lot of claims, but where's the evidence?

A strong interviewer will keep pushing you for facts: What exactly did you do? How did you do it? What happened? What did you learn? Less proficient interviewers won't do this, so you will have to supply this evidence anyway.

Beginners in the job search game use clichés, saying they are *self-starters* or *team players*. Others list more developed characteristics and throw in bigger claims (*'highly motivated'*, *'a born winner'*). **Average** candidates make claims, but they are often unsubstantiated: *'I am highly experienced at customer service.'* **Strong** candidates offer detailed supporting evidence – hard evidence from their work history. Chapter 6 offers more ideas on packaging your best evidence.

'Yes, I have experience of supervising others under pressure. Last summer I managed a team of temps who sold our products in an exhibition tent. I was the

only company representative there so I had to show them how to demonstrate products, give them advice on customer service, and deal with the more difficult queries.'

✳Q83 Tell me about a major project you've worked on recently

Discuss a project that is sufficiently complex and where your personal contribution is very clear. This is a good topic for a well-rehearsed summary. Plan to talk about a recent project that shows you in a good light, has a clear beginning, middle, and end:

'A good example is where my manager asked me to rewrite our training pack for new staff. I negotiated a deadline and also delegated some tasks to create the time to complete the job. I had to consult five team leaders, but also checked things out with one or two people who had been through the induction process recently. I rewrote about 50 per cent of the material, and after the next induction course we got a much improved score on the quality of materials.'

✳Q84 What difference will you make in your first 90 days?

Recruitment specialists often talk about the critical first three months in a role. Michael Watkins suggests in *The First 90 Days* (Harvard Business School Press) that up to 50 per cent of external appointments fail to achieve the desired results, and this is perfectly clear within 90 days. Be clear about where you could make the biggest impact in the role. Drill down into job information to work out the employer's number one problem. If you have established the key facts, put forward a realistic answer. If you have a 'been there, done that' experience, now is the time to highlight it.

If you are asked about changes or improvements you would make, do some careful balancing. Too many candidates go for a safe answer (*'I won't change anything until I learn a lot more about the job and the perspective of colleagues'*). This can sound like slow progress. On the other hand, employers are rightly suspicious of candidates who have instant-fix solutions without understanding the organisation – and barriers to success. So, anything that sounds like *'I'd be a breath of fresh air!'* will fall on sceptical ears – too many candidates over-promise and under-deliver.

The employer is imagining what you'd be like in the role. Be careful what you suggest – you may pick on a problem area which is the brainchild of someone in the room. If the employer points to clear problems that need solving, then you can offer solutions. Unless the organisation is explicitly looking for immediate turnaround, find a midpoint position which conveys the subtext: *'I will consult carefully enough not to tread on toes, but I will also get things moving quickly.'* Suggest experiments and pilot schemes, or say *'In a previous role I had some success with. . .'.* Present your proposed strategy as something open to discussion, rather than a fixed plan. Offer quick wins that can be obtained with little investment or disruption:

'I've got some ideas for procurement cost savings you might achieve, based on my last role – I'd really like to get to grips with your purchase ledger. . .'

You may be asked how long will it take you to make a meaningful contribution. If the timescale you suggest is too extended, interviewers wonder if you will ever have an impact. Since organisations are worried about their return on investment, don't extend the time frame beyond six months. On the other hand, saying *'From day one'* requires solid detail.

Top 10 tips for excelling at telephone interviews

1. Find a quiet room to take the call without any interruptions or background noise (never try to undertake an interview from a train or in a public place).
2. If you take the call at your desk, turn your computer OFF, otherwise you will easily be distracted by incoming email while you speak.
3. Have in front of you the same information you would take into an interview. You won't have time to look up documents for extra information – print important items in advance.
4. Accept any invitation for small talk at the beginning and the end of the interview as this is your only chance to build a relationship.
5. Be sure you know the name of the person interviewing you and use that name from time to time.
6. Be prepared for unscheduled calls. Keep a list on hand of people likely to call.
7. If the interviewer calls unexpectedly, gather your thoughts and take the call if you can. If not, ask for a 15-minute delay.

8. When you answer the phone, announce your name with enthusiasm, and don't start sounding flat, or as if you've been interrupted.
9. Make occasional notes to keep you focused on the exact wording of questions.
10. For added confidence, take the phone call standing up.

10

Showcasing your competencies

COMPRESSING YOUR BEST EVIDENCE

Past predicts future

As we've identified, with practice you can anticipate most interview questions. Some questions are less predictable (oddball questions are covered in Chapter 11). Most questions relate to the needs of the organisation. Yes, there may be questions you hope to avoid, but you can be certain you'll be asked questions which dig deep to understand past performance.

Employers want to know what you can do, but a bare list of skills doesn't say enough – CVs don't come to work, people do. Accurately predicting workplace performance is notoriously problematic. Skills are difficult enough to measure before someone starts in the job, but what an interviewer really wants to know is *how* you use a skill – the skill level you achieve, your working style, and (the all-important factor outlined in Chapter 8) your *attitude. How* includes motivation and attitude – do you work quickly, purposefully, creatively? Do you spot better ways of working and recommend them to others? Do you go out of your way to help?

This is one of the reasons that many professional interviewers look at **competencies**. A competency is your unique blend of know-how, skills, and attitude. For example, handling a customer order by email requires background knowledge (of codes, systems, products) and skills in data management and written communication. Competencies are sometimes described as 'performance behaviours' – observable actions which create measurable results. Organisational theorist Richard Boyatzis defined a competency as 'an underlying characteristic of an individual which is causally related to *effective or superior performance*'. Note the italics – competency means not just having skills, but putting them into action in an above-average way. Look, for example, at the competency of 'providing excellent customer service to telephone enquiries'. A competent operator will be able to answer a phone within a prescribed number of rings and deal efficiently with a customer. An above-average performer will make the call feel like a good experience for the customer.

One way of understanding the idea is that it creates a rounded, detailed picture of how you behave at work – helping to predict future work performance. For example, your CV may list the skill 'handling customer complaints'. Even if an employer asked you to role play this ability, that still wouldn't reveal how you act in real situations. Your past is where the evidence lies.

Competency (or behavioural) interviews look for tangible evidence of past behaviours. A traditional interview might focus just on relevant work roles you've held before, but a competency interview asks you to supply evidence of past situations, problems and challenges, and how you handled them. This gives you the opportunity to talk about any part of your experience where you might have displayed the required competency, including volunteering or activities outside work.

You will usually see clear indications where an employer is examining competencies. They will probably be listed in job documents. You may receive instructions to provide competency evidence in your application form or at interview. For example, you may read: '*At interview you will be expected to give detailed examples of where you have demonstrated listed competencies.*' Where you see directions like this, prepare carefully structured evidence. For example, in a customer services role you will talk about skills *and* attitude (e.g. calming the situation with an irate customer, information gathering, displaying empathy, spending time to listen, offering solutions).

Other competencies frequently seen in a wide range of roles include:

- The ability to meet deadlines (see **Q50**).
- The ability to make decisions under pressure (**Q40**).
- Problem-solving in complex situations (**Q87**).
- A capacity to learn the job quickly and deliver results (**Q84** and **Q118**).
- The ability to cope with difficult customers (see **Q106**).
- The ability to manage projects (**Q49**).
- The ability to achieve goals (**Q71**, **Q84**, and **Q93**).
- Managing people (**Q94–Q99**).

Unpacking competencies

If you find yourself applying for a role where competencies will be measured, complete the **Competency Checklist** below. You can spot the key competencies for a job in a number of ways:

- Where specific competencies are listed in the job description (it is also useful to dig deeper in documentation and work out what things really matter to the hiring organisation). You may be asked to provide a written statement matching your evidence against each competency, in which case you can use this chapter to help you construct good written examples.

- Where the job description and advertisement talk about a mix of skills, knowledge, and attitudes; again, preparing competency-based evidence is useful here too.
- Where the job is defined in terms of activities, targets, or outcomes – work back from those to establish what kind of behaviours will be needed to achieve them.

Prepare evidence against all competencies listed. However, you can anticipate that some will matter more than others. Scrutinise the job documentation to work out which competencies are going to be most important. Some things (for example, background IT skills or knowledge of certain work systems) may be relevant but less important.

On the **Competency Checklist** give *marginal* competencies (nice to have but not terribly important) a score of 1. Identify the competencies that seem to be *vital* ('must have' ingredients, core parts of the job, likely to be big ticket items at interview). Give them a high score of 3. Give a score of 2 to everything else in the middle – the things that are important, but perhaps not the primary items on the employer shopping list.

Now turn your attention to the right-hand column. List your key experiences, using bullet points to remind you about the mini-narratives you need to prepare before a competency-based interview.

Competency Checklist		
Position:		
Competencies required	**Ranking** 3 = Vital 2 = Important 1 = Marginal	**Key experiences** (Bullet point reminders of times you used these competencies)

Keep it fresh, keep it real

The main reason for competency questions is to drill into actual experience, so don't fall into the same trap as many candidates talking about what you 'usually' do. Some panels will listen in silence and afterwards will agree that you failed to answer properly. Provide concrete examples: talk about one project, one task, one day. Keeping it real isn't just about being honest – your material needs to sound credible, too. For example, claiming you changed company policy might be true, but you've got to give enough detail for the story to be convincing.

Anyone conducting this kind of interview regularly will tell you that answers often sound robotic, over-rehearsed, and yawn-inducing. Candidates learn statements to match the (highly predictable) questions beginning 'Tell me about a time when. . .', and they sound like someone reading the telephone directory. When you're unpacking a competency you've got a wonderful opportunity for storytelling (see **Energy and storytelling** in Chapter 8).

Q85   What competencies were required for your last job?

Be careful not to throw this gift question away or think it's too easy to prepare for. Too frequently, interviewers are more interested in screening out rather than screening in, *and this question could be the decision maker*. Talk about your most important responsibilities or the aspects that provided you with the most visibility. Don't list competencies in a dull way – talk enthusiastically about ways you exceeded expectations, packing your answer with appropriate evidence:

'I had to be good at writing and editing effective web pieces under time pressure, understanding the needs of our audience at all times. For example. . .'

*★Q86   Where exactly have you used this competency?

This is the way most behavioural questions are constructed. Take no chances, prepare thorough answers in advance. Learn a series of mini-narratives to communicate:

- The problem or situation you had to deal with.
- What you, personally, did in response – focusing on your competencies.
- The outcome or result you achieved.

'I used attention to detail when I was given the task of editing all of our tender documents into a single ring binder, with each document following the house style, and all cross-references and figures double-checked.'

Q87 Describe a complex problem you've had to handle recently

To prepare an answer to this question, refer back to your **Experience Catalogue** (page 72) and **Key Turning Points Worksheet** (page 97). Select a strong example where you worked with a problem which was reasonably complex. For the word 'problem' substitute 'project' if it helps to clarify appropriate situations.

'I've handled a number of complex problems in the last couple of months. One example would be the IT support behind setting up a centralised accounting function. My first task was to write the project planning document, and to do this I had to interview all the departmental heads to find out exactly what they needed and when. Next I had to put together a specification so that we could put the technical side out to tender. . .'

'Our department had always struggled with the quality of temps we received from local recruitment agencies. I was able to build on my previous HR experience to do two things: tighten up the quality of agency pre-screening, and building our own small pool of regulars.'

Be aware of **timelines**. *The longer the timeframe between the start of a project and its completion, the* *greater the responsibility.* Lower-level personnel may deal with daily pressures and deadlines; higher management looks to longer-range projects and deadlines. Position your response accordingly.

Q88   What part do you normally play in a team?

This is a natural follow-up question on teams. Don't be satisfied with the generalised term 'team player'. When we talk about 'team players', most people mean those who are naturally extrovert and who display leadership characteristics, but there are many different roles in successful teams. You might be a natural leader, or someone who persuades others to work together. You might be an idea builder, a good organiser, or a safe pair of hands – someone who ensures projects are completed on time.

Often candidates say 'we' rather than 'I' when talking about team accomplishments. That's fine for a while, but do make it crystal clear what *you* contributed to any team. Were you the ideas person, the coordinator, the project driver? Or perhaps you were the person who stopped the other members of the team strangling each other?

✱Q89   Tell me about a time when you worked in an effective team

All team questions are opportunities to show how well you understand teams, and where you have made strong contributions. Learn how to 'set the scene' for this kind of answer. If you spend too long giving an overview of why the team was formed and what the team did, you will lose the interviewer's attention. Give the background quickly. Mention in particular if the team included a mix in terms of disciplines or seniority, and be sure to say what you brought to the party:

'I was part of a multidisciplinary team looking at the customer experience. My role was to give a chalkface perspective and show what our customers actually think and feel when they come into our stores. Many of my colleagues in marketing and distribution hadn't thought about that perspective before, and took some wining over. As a result, we brought in a brand-new training module and some very different point-of-sale materials.'

Q90   Tell me about a time when you were in a team which wasn't functioning well

Here's a question which lures you into talking about relationship difficulties. Be realistic; you have of course worked in difficult teams or with awkward people, and you have a range of approaches in your toolkit to help when this happens:

'When I was a student I found temporary work with a distribution company. I had problems from the start because I wanted to show how productive I could be. Every day, even though I was new, I was setting productivity records. The union steward, and then a few of my fellow workers, let me know in very direct language that my work habits needed to change or I would encounter difficulty in my work relationships. Even my supervisor felt the need to tell me to slow down. I felt it was diplomatic to find work in another department where the work was faster-paced.'

Teamworking is a highly regarded competency in a variety of work contexts, so you need to show that you are an active and cooperative team member. Don't just say it, show it. Tell a story that includes progress or improvement:

'I was part of the team which scoped out the new building, and at first we didn't make much progress. People complained that our goals were unclear, but it struck me that the real reason we weren't making progress was that we hadn't got to know each other well enough and no one felt confident saying what they really felt. So we organised a fact-finding trip to another building and made sure this included a pub lunch, which broke the ice nicely.'

You may be probed about a time when you improved the way a team was working. Identify a situation where your personal intervention led to a positive outcome (be careful to mix 'we' and 'I' to demonstrate that you were an active participant of the group but also made a distinctive contribution):

'We had to cut back from six to four staff members in our project team, even though our workload was increasing. We decided to meet to map out a strategy to determine how we were going to accomplish the same results with only four people. For the next two days I visited each person (including the departing employees) to hear both their concerns and their ideas for ways forward. In our strategy meeting we had five minutes of negativity, but because we had already discussed ideas for moving forward we quickly rolled our sleeves up to create an action plan.'

Q91 Tell me about a time when you were in a team failing to achieve its goals

Most candidates prefer to give problem-free examples of times when things went perfectly and outcomes were achieved. A good interviewer will probe for times when things didn't go well. You won't be believed if you say *'Every team I have worked in has been successful.'* Show the interviewer that you have strategies which work if you are part of a team that is underperforming. Your answer will first show that you can spot team problems before they become major issues, and second that you are able do something about them.

'One of our team responsibilities was finding a way to integrate two departments. The problem was that the team was composed of members of staff from both companies, and no one wanted to give an inch. We resolved this by using a clever visual model, using 'red' and 'green' to describe the different functions, and deliberately seeking solutions that were a win/win for each side of the equation.'

Positive team contributions

- Accepting responsibility for problems.
- Encouraging other team members.
- Keeping other team members 'in the loop'.
- Supporting decisions (even when you're not happy about them).
- Sharing success and not allocating blame.
- Being optimistic in tough situations.

Q92 Tell me about a time when you had to persuade someone to do something they were unhappy about

Prepare an answer which shows that you can get things done without being over-directive or manipulating the result:

'*A graduate we hired needed to be reminded that her responsibilities included answering the telephone and dealing with general enquiries. During the selection process we had emphasised that the 'hands-on' culture of our organisation meant she would have to take on basic duties from time to time. I realised that the best way of tackling this problem was to reinforce the idea that she needed to do what other members of the team do. Introduced this way, the request was accepted.*'

Q93 Tell us about a time when you failed to reach a goal

You've prepared for questions about goals you've achieved, so it's reasonable to expect questions about misses as well as hits. Interviewers want to know how you deal with setbacks, and also if you can adapt your approach if things don't seem to be working. Describe a time at work when you had to adjust your sights, regroup, and you got a win further down the line. If your interviewer is interested in resilience (see **Q58**) show how you keep motivated in tough times. It can be useful to refer to failures that were outside your control but helped to bring a team together, or provided a learning experience:

'*I was asked by a client to design a programme for training internal recruiters. Many meetings were held, with senior management requesting revisions which I accommodated. The meetings never resulted in a signed contract, because the HR manager left in the middle of negotiations to work for a competitor. However, it gave me a real insight into the needs of the business, and we eventually designed a training programme that we were able to sell on to some of our other HR clients.'*

✱Q94 Why do you feel you have management potential?

You may be after a job which is the first rung on the management ladder, but you have little management experience or training. It won't help if you simply state that you have always wanted to be a manager. You will, no doubt, have some experience of supervising, informing, training, coaching, or supporting others – this is what you draw on so that **evidence reveals potential**. Seek even stronger evidence if you can – for example, where you took responsibility for a project or task, or deputised for a manager.

'We had a dozen temps in and it was my job to show them how to scan documents for electronic filing. I wrote out a sheet with key instructions set out, but also explained it on a one-to-one basis and dealt with queries and problems.'

'I was asked to represent my department at a recent meeting chaired by the FD. I consulted colleagues on their views, wrote a short report, spoke about it at the meeting, and brought comments back to my boss and the rest of the team. The feedback was that I had done a good job representing the team's views diplomatically.'

Q95 What's the most difficult thing you've had to do as a manager?

If you have managerial experience, employers want evidence that you've got to grips with the tougher aspects of the job. Examples might include telling someone they are underperforming, saying no to a request for promotion, issuing a verbal warning, or telling someone they are going to be made redundant. Show you're not afraid of tackling difficult tasks, but you can act tactfully.

'Since I was in charge of the unit, I was responsible for the annual review of staff members. Generally, people were reasonably well motivated, but I had one individual who was always late for work, and I had to go through a formal process of warnings with him which eventually led to his termination. I was always very straight and open with him and, on the day he left, he thanked me for my patience.'

Q96 What do you see as the hardest part of being a manager?

(See also **Q99** on leadership qualities.) The interviewer seems to be asking for your opinion, but is in fact probing your track record. As with **Q95**, your answer is going to have to deal with the more demanding parts of the role – accepting responsibility, dealing with difficult situations or people, having to drive people to improve their performance. Demonstrate the depth of your experience and your ability to take on the more difficult aspects of the role.

'Giving bad news' is a succinct answer, but be prepared to give an example of where you have done this. Alternatively, think about an example which shows that, as a manager, you're ready to take control and provide leadership from the start:

'Getting the group of people that you have inherited to respond quickly and effectively to your authority.'

Prepare for a range of questions on how you manage people. There are many styles of management, but you will, of course, be matching your personal style carefully with the style and needs of the organisation interviewing you. A manager needs to find a balance between task outcomes and people outcomes. Some of your time is spent building people up, developing them, shaping them; and some of your time is about influencing people so what they do is on time and on target:

'I've had managers who talked about having an open door, but they were never in their offices. I make sure I spend some time every day walking about, picking up the vibe and giving people a chance to catch me early with problems or suggestions.'

Q97 Tell me about a time when you had to make a tough management decision

Match the level of decision-making to the role on offer. A senior buyer may readily mention handling contracts worth millions, while an assembly line worker may talk about the authority to shut the line down. Say something about the level of the decision you had to make, why it was difficult, and who you consulted; but be sure you emphasise that you made a decision and stuck to it. The interviewer is in reality probing difficulties you might have making decisions under pressure, so be prepared for a follow-up question.

'My toughest decision was dropping a supplier we had been trading with for 30 years. They had become complacent, and twice they supplied parts that weren't fit for purpose. I warned them they were under scrutiny,

but they didn't take me seriously, and a decision had to be made. I felt bad about it because I knew people would lose their jobs, but I had to do my job.'

Ensure your answer shows you can review a situation, exercise control, organise, and give a clear sense of direction:

'Relocation expenses were out of control when I took responsibility for the function. I worked with experienced staff to determine where we were spending money carelessly. My team gave me a series of recommendations and I commissioned them to draft new guidelines. We then set up a workflow system to make sure that a new policy was published and implemented.'

If you have only ever managed volunteers, show how you persuaded them to achieve results; managing volunteers can be more demanding than managing paid staff. Think about situations where you had to manage people or resources, sort out a problem, or give a group of people instructions, encouragement, or a sense of direction.

Q98 How do you communicate with people above you in the organisation?

Show you can present information with clarity and confidence to top-level staff, but also that you can communicate to your peers and direct reports as well:

'I mentioned an idea in passing to the MD, and he asked me to make an appointment to see him the next day to explain it in detail. I knew he doesn't like

excessive detail, so I made sure I had thought through the advantages and disadvantages of my proposal, and set them out clearly in a brief summary document. I got him to say 'yes' in five minutes, and I got to be in charge of the project.'

Q99 Where have you displayed leadership qualities?

Leadership, in the eyes of recruiters, is a variable quality. In general terms, managers work within set parameters and resources, and deliver against organisational targets. Leaders tend to expand boundaries, create new opportunities, and rewrite the rules when they face new situations. Perhaps the strongest characteristic of leaders is their ability to influence. Leaders communicate effectively, and often, conveying a strong sense of vision and encouraging others to follow. Decide through your homework which qualities are most useful in this job context:

'I think you have plenty of people around who can manage people and resources, but I think a leader needs to inspire others and give them exciting goals. For example. . .'

'As a leader in the charity world I recognise that you have to keep reminding people of the reasons they come to work, and show them how they are making a difference.'

Leadership attributes

- Decision-making (particularly under tough conditions).
- Setting visionary goals.

- Redefining what the organisation does.
- Exploring new territory.
- Launching new products or ideas.
- Inspiring staff to improve their performance.
- Consulting with direct reports to understand their perspective and opinions.
- Keeping colleagues committed and focused.

Matching your experience to the evidence

Even when it comes to basic competencies, make sure your examples have enough detail. For example, if you are talking about filing as a competency, identify a time when you dealt with something difficult or unusual. When writing competency statements or getting prepared to talk about them at interview, think about the time sequence behind your examples. Where did you begin? What steps did you take? What did *you* do? The **four-step competency flow chart** below will help you to formulate your evidence:

Four-step competency flow chart

1   Situation: What problem did you face? What obstacles did you have to overcome?

2   Action: What did you actually do?

3   Outcome: What was the result?

4   Learning: What did you learn from the experience? What would you do differently if you were to do this again?

So, if I could just summarise. . .

You may hear an interviewer summarising some of the things you say. This can helpfully reveal what's been heard and understood. Listen carefully – you will pick up interesting clues about what the interviewer has given most attention to. Reinforce information that is correct, affirm the quality of a good summary, and don't be timid about correcting a misunderstanding:

'That captures things nicely, but may I just add that although I am not currently in a B2B role I have in the past built sales with a number of small business contacts.'

Take this as a welcome opportunity to add vital information:

'Perhaps it would be helpful if I add that I also had purchasing responsibility in my first job – I had to put together the company's first preferred suppliers list.'

'We haven't talked much yet about my experience of social media. I designed a multi-channel campaign this year that went viral on Twitter.'

Top 10 tips for discussing your competencies

1. **Listen**: Pick up clues about how the interviewer sees the competency.
2. **Be objective**: get to know yourself better. Seek feedback from trusted colleagues about what you are good at, and your normal working style.
3. Answer with pre-prepared **short stories**; do not ramble.
4. Don't **generalise** – give concrete examples of what you have actually done.
5. Use **appropriate language** – avoid jargon.
6. **Break it down** – situation, contribution, and result.
7. Think about underlying **attitude** – *how* you used your skills.
8. Talk about **team working**, but emphasise your personal contribution.
9. Prepare detailed evidence where you believe your CV underplays important **competencies**.
10. Ensure **coverage** – talk about all parts of the competency described.

11

Difficult and wildcard questions

CAN YOU TAKE THE HEAT?

There are many things that add to interview stress. Although you will normally be sent directions about where, when, and how the interview will take place, things can go wrong for reasons outside your control. You may be delayed in your journey. You may be asked to wait while an earlier interview overruns, or discover that the 'friendly chat' is actually a panel interview.

The better your preparation, the easier it is to cope when things go off track. Decide in advance that at least one of these events is going to happen, and when it does, don't let it distract you from your interview plan. Last-minute adjustments to your strategy are usually dangerous. Examples include cutting big chunks from a well-crafted presentation (see Chapter 9), failing to make key points at the end of the interview, or introducing new material you haven't road-tested. Don't be pushed into improvising – it will take you into unexplored minefields.

An interview is designed to take you in two directions simultaneously – relaxing you enough to get you to disclose information, but also applying enough pressure to test your answers. When the pressure's on it feels personal. You don't just feel your experience is being measured – you feel judged as a person. That's why it makes no sense if someone says 'It's only an interview.' Even hardened sales people can find it difficult to talk about themselves. Don't beat yourself up if you find interviews stressful. Most people do.

One of the ways of anticipating stress is to plan for the fact that occasionally you'll be asked questions designed to upset your equilibrium. We live in two different worlds simultaneously. In the first world interviewers use objective questions to extract evidence which predicts workplace performance. In the second, interviewers ask questions which have little obvious relationship to the job – questions which deliberately throw you off balance.

Oddball questions

There are fashions in question style. From time to time employers come up with new selection ideas – for example, asking a candidate to tell a joke, sing a song, or perform mental gymnastics. In 2016, applicants to one Oxford University college were asked 'If you could invent a new musical instrument, what kind of sound would it make?' Employers can be equally creative. Questions like this can pop up with no warning. They can sound absurd or puzzling; you may even wonder if the interviewer is making a strange joke.

Interviewers ask wildcard questions for a range of reasons. A bored interviewer may throw one in just to spice things up or to test your sense of humour. Some mistakenly believe that these questions reveal your 'true' personality under pressure. Whatever the reason, they keep coming. They can sometimes be clever, more relevant than they seem, and can lead to interesting answers. Consult the Internet for examples. Take the question 'What's on your mantelpiece at home?' Your answer could be about family photographs, sports trophies, art objects you treasure, invitations to social events. One candidate replied: *'dust'*.

Try to respond with good humour. Don't get flustered, because the only wrong response is to freeze like a rabbit in the headlights. Keep your answer light. Think of them rather like the light-hearted 'and finally' questions that are sometimes asked in the closing minutes of television debate programmes such as *Question Time*. There is a swift change of tone as the topic changes from tax policy to the MP's favourite TV soap, and we get to see a slightly more 'off duty' personality. Employers are looking for the same revealing effect.

Once you have had a few interviews you will discover that interviewers ask a very wide range of questions, some of them strange, all exacting:

Q100 If you were an animal in the jungle, what animal would you be?

If you are asked this kind of question, keep a sense of humour. Respond with a smile, perhaps saying *'You must get some interesting answers to that question'*, or you might answer in the same style: *'The biggest one.'*

Sadly, there are still many employers out there who believe in the value of fantasy questions – off-the-wall questions which can throw unwary candidates. Here are some of the stranger questions that have been asked:

- If you were a car, what kind of car would you be?
- What's the best way to nail jelly to a ceiling?
- Who in the world would you like to have lunch with?
- If you were a biscuit, what kind of biscuit would you like to be?

- What would you like to be written on your gravestone?
- What would you do if you won the lottery?

Questions like this certainly test your inventiveness. Some interviewers believe they bring out the liveliest, sharpest candidates. The reason that professional recruiters avoid such questions is that they can be seen as unfair, they provide poor evidence of likely workplace performance, and have little or nothing to do with the job.

Can you prepare for this kind of question? Yes. Look at job content. Will you need quick thinking? Improvisation? Good-natured responses to difficult enquiries? Is it the kind of role that requires lateral thinking, mental arithmetic, or logical problem-solving? Further questions probing these abilities are covered below. Practising short, good-humoured responses will help, but keep a 'play for time' response up your sleeve:

'Wow – great question. While I'm digging around for a good answer, tell me – how do people usually answer that?'

Q101 If you were going to Mars, what three things would you take?

Sometimes questions like this are used to seek evidence of your ability to think creatively under pressure. Don't let the question floor you even if it really bothers you – don't let the interviewer see that you are easily rattled. Best not to take the answer too seriously:

'Oh, it's one of those questions. Let me see. A good book. A clockwork torch to read with at night. And a map of Mars, perhaps. What would you take?'

'My mind always goes blank when I get that kind of question and I think of a great answer on the way home. Are you thinking of things that would be useful, or things that would be fun?'

Q102 If our roles were reversed, what questions would you ask?

The answer *'You've covered everything thoroughly'* is rather weak and avoids the playful spirit of the question. It is really trying to probe how well you understand the role. Don't suggest a question which would floor you, but suggest a question which takes you to the top half-dozen or so points you want to get across. Ensure it's a question about the things in the job that really matter, and one which affords you the opportunity to give a strong and confident answer:

'In your shoes I'd want to be sure that I have the customer service experience required by this role. I believe that my varied experience shows you. . .'

Failing that, go for *'What can you do for us?'* or *'Why do you want to join our organisation?'* as these are gift questions if you're a well-prepared interviewee, and show that you are confident enough to answer the most direct questions.

This is also a chance to slip in a question that you really want to be asked because you have an excellent response that will set you up against the opposition:

'In your position I'd ask why, in a strong field of candidates, I should get the job. My answer is that I have not only the right track record and proven skills, but I am a huge fan of your product range.'

Q103   What's 17% of £40,000?

If you know that the job requires the ability to calculate figures quickly during a negotiation, then you need to show what you would actually do in the workplace:

'Let me tell you how I deal with pricing. I know the answer is just short of £7,000, but I never respond to a price request without double-checking on a calculator. That way, I avoid mistakes, and I get time to think if the deal is a good one. So – do you have a calculator?'

However, if you know that the job requires good mental arithmetic, get it right. Weaker candidates calculate quickly and, even though they are normally fairly good at juggling numbers in their heads, get it wrong. Better to check before speaking. One technique is to calculate out loud but make it sound like you are simply checking the first figure that came to mind:

'OK – let me just double-check. 10% is £4,000, 15% is £6,000, add an extra 2% which is £800, the total is 6,800.'

Q104   How many light bulbs are there in this building?

This might not be an off-the-wall question but one which seeks out your ability to make assumptions and estimate quickly:

'I can see six or so in this room, which takes up about one-tenth of this floor. You have 10 floors. You probably have a lot more lights per square foot in reception and in corridors, so let's say 700. Am I close?'

A variation on this question is 'How much soap is sold in the UK annually?' – candidates need to estimate based on population and the longevity of a soap bar.

Q105 Sell me this stapler

If you've applied for a job as a book-keeper, this is a fantasy question which is unlikely to distinguish top performers in a role. However, if your role involves selling, particularly the kind of sales role that requires you to think on your feet, this kind of role play is far from rare. Anticipate. Think about how you would sell those items likely to be within the interviewer's grasp (pencil, paper clip, stapler, coaster, etc.). Perform a quick analysis – features and benefits. At the drop of a hat, be prepared to list three of each:

'This stapler is small enough to take up the tiniest space on your desk, stylish enough to match your image, and powerful enough to do the job. This stapler is always easy to find, makes you look good, and does the job. You need this stapler.'

Does that sound like improvised comedy? Of course it does – this kind of role play is closer to stand-up than a real occupational assessment. However, several things are being communicated: you can think on your feet, you sound confident, you can sell, and all with a smile. People buy from people, ideally from people they like, so you're doing all the right things, even if it isn't actually a realistic scenario.

One simple sales technique is to quickly get your target to say 'yes' as many times as possible – 'yes' to the need for a stapler, 'yes' to the fact that it will make his life easier, 'yes' to the fact that this stapler is both useful and attractive, and 'yes' to your proposition that it's excellent value for money. Play it tongue in cheek, but play to win (see also **Q46**).

Q106 How would you deal with an angry customer?

We've looked at eccentric questions which sometimes take you beyond reality. However, this one is *not* a fantasy question. It's a demanding question, but it's rooted in the context of the role – the things a postholder will actually experience. Most of us from time to time will have to deal with awkward, angry, and even abusive customers. It's not just a hypothetical question ('What would you do if. . .?'). Assuming it's based on the actual job, it's a reasonable question replicating a typical problem.

Don't take an awkward line with this kind of question; saying *'It depends. . .'* simply irritates. Also, don't generalise by saying *'I think it's important to. . .'* or *'What I would do is. . .'.* Dip into genuine experience. Give an answer which shows that you have dealt with this before and you're ready to do so again:

'The best way to answer that is to give you a real example. I was manning an exhibition stand when a customer came up to me and ranted about being overcharged. The first thing I did was. . .'

Q107 Where does your boss think you are right now?

This is a nasty (and thankfully rare) question, and of course applies only to those who are currently in work and have taken time out for a job interview. Don't use it as an excuse to vent your feelings about your boss (*'I don't know and I don't care'*). Communicating disloyalty and a willingness to deceive will not endear you to a potential employer, and nor will dishonesty (*'I said I had a dental appointment'*). Go for an answer which shows professionalism and also that you take your job search seriously.

'I always take part of my annual leave when I have an interview to give myself plenty of time to focus.'

Legal and decent

Employers 'discriminate' every day, in the true sense of the word, which is 'to choose'. UK recruitment law requires employers to choose the best person for the job. Additionally, various codes of practice encourage employers to operate fair and open selection policies. Interviewers are not allowed to ask questions which directly or indirectly discriminate against you on various grounds, which include race, racial origin, sexual orientation, gender, marital status, disability, age, religious belief, trade union membership, and whistle-blowing. Employers can and do gather information about gender and race, but this information is gathered to help monitor diversity, and should not be used when making a hiring decision.

Interviewers sometimes ask illegal questions out of ignorance, sometimes out of arrogance. A minority take pleasure in asking unpleasant or unacceptable questions (thankfully, this kind of dinosaur is now a fairly rare beast). There are innumerable questions you may hear which are discourteous, unprofessional, and irrelevant, even if they are entirely lawful. However, most of the questions which follow here are unlawful as well as unacceptable.

Remember, you have legal obligations too. Any information you include in an application form or CV must be honest. If it isn't, your employer may have grounds to dismiss you without notice.

What to do if you're asked an illegal question

Sometimes it's hard to know if a question breaks the law, or is just simply inappropriate. You may decide to make a note of the question and think about it afterwards. You may wish to make a formal complaint. You have the legal right to take an employer to an Industrial Tribunal if you feel that that the interview process treated you unfairly, or the selection decision was made unlawfully. This is your right, but be aware that it will involve a great deal of your time and energy. Organisations that insist on asking illegal questions are often not great places to work.

Unlawful questions are still asked, more often than you might think. If you don't want to answer, say so politely. Pulling an interviewer up on a question which you may feel is illegal will almost certainly damage any rapport that exists. A compromise position (suggested by several example answers below) is to offer a mild challenge (after all, you may not be 100 per cent sure if the question is illegal) and to reframe it through your answer, bringing the focus back to the job on offer.

Q108 How do you feel about working with a female boss?

This question is almost never asked about a male boss, and it's clearly sexist. It's probably best not to provide a critique of how unprofessional the question sounds, but just give a quick response that reinforces the overall impression that you are flexible:

'I'm happy working with a good boss, male or female. Although all of my bosses have been men, I've often had to work alongside senior female managers from other departments.'

Q109 This job requires long hours. Will this be a problem in terms of family commitments?

This question discriminates against women – it's rarely asked of men. You may choose not to answer, or to indicate that you find the question inappropriate or discriminatory. If you choose to answer, once again focus on the needs of the job. The precise details of how you propose to manage childcare are not the concern of your employer.

'I believe I don't have to answer that question. My track record clearly shows that I've always managed both a home and a job. What is the commitment here in terms of travel and nights away from home?'

The interviewer should be focusing on the actual requirements of the job, and not making assumptions about any restrictions on your working hours which might or might not arise from family obligations. Employers should state the requirements of the job, including the hours you may need to be available, any unsocial hours, any travel or nights away from home.

'I'm happy to work the hours required.'

Q110 You last worked 12 years ago. How up to date are your skills?

This question is potentially discriminatory because it will probably be asked more of women returners than of other jobseekers. However, although an employer cannot discriminate unfairly against women returners, you don't get any special advantage; you still need to prove you can do the job. Remember that although a question like this is unprofessional, it does reveal a concern that your skills may be out of date – and possibly a prejudice that you're only looking for a job to pay bills rather than seeking a developed career:

'While I have not been in paid work for a while, I have extensive voluntary experience, working with the homeless and also at the family drop-in centre. At first I was involved in frontline roles which gave me valuable experience of dealing with a very wide range of people who were often angry or upset. Two years ago I was made manager at the centre which has given me a much broader range of skills including supervising volunteers, managing a budget, and keeping extensive records.'

Ensure your CV and interview performance include plenty of evidence of the ways you have kept your skills current and relevant:

'You're probably concerned that I don't have the latest IT skills. I can tell you that for the last two years I've been honorary treasurer for my local golf club and kept computerised accounts using all the latest software. I have been on refresher courses on Photoshop and PowerPoint, which I know are required in this role . . . I think my skills are pretty up to date.'

Q111 Don't you think you're a little too old/young for this job?

Age discrimination is illegal in the UK. Employers are discouraged from asking your age or date of birth, and not allowed to make appointment decisions based on this information. In reality, employers want details about the date you obtained qualifications or undertook training, and the start and end dates for jobs. As a result, they usually have a fairly good idea of your age.

Some jobs (particularly in publishing, PR, media, and more recently teaching) are clearly in 'young' cultures (often because long hours are combined with low pay). You may be brave enough to push for such sectors. However, if you're old enough to remember Prime Ministers before Tony Blair, you might be better focusing on sectors and organisations which value maturity, steadiness, and depth of knowledge. You can't keep your age a secret in the recruitment process, but don't make an issue of it or draw attention to it. If the topic comes up in interview, play to your strengths:

'I think I have maturity and experience that younger applicants are missing. Besides, they'll be off in two years, but I'm looking for a long-term position.'

You may be considered too young for a role. Sometimes picking the best person for the job will inevitably mean choosing someone with experience, which favours older candidates. Some employers are looking for a degree of 'gravitas' and maturity. Even so, younger applicants can sometimes surprise the field by getting the job – if they can demonstrate they have the maturity and confidence to hold down a demanding role:

'*You might be surprised to hear that I've been supervising people since I was 17 years old. I have no problem supervising older workers or making tough decisions, for example. . .*'

Most younger applicants rely on personality and an optimistic sense of their potential. If you have actual evidence, use it.

Q112   Can you do this job with your health problem?

It is legal for an employer to ask if you have health issues which affect your ability to work (a 'disability' as far as employment law is concerned is a significant long-term health condition that limits your working capacity). However, it is illegal to discriminate on the grounds of disability. The law in this area is complex, and operates around what is 'reasonable' for an employer. If you are a jobseeker with long-term health issues, take specialist advice (see www.disabilityrightsuk.org).

Top 10 tips for handling difficult questions

1. Deal with difficult questions in advance. Use this book to anticipate problem questions and typical oddball questions.

2. Anticipate the worst. Think about where you are vulnerable, and what kinds of questions might throw you in the interview room.

3. Avoid going on the defensive or thinking too much. A light-hearted response shows you're happy to play the game.

4. Ask questions to clarify need and give yourself thinking time – for example: 'Has this been a major problem?'

5. Think about the interviewer's reason for asking the question.

6. Keep your cool. Fidgeting and other symptoms of discomfort may make the interviewer feel you have something to hide or that you will not be up to the pressure of the job.

7. Slow it down. Don't blurt out an answer just to move on to another topic. Speak calmly.

8. Appear to welcome probing questions. If you seem uncomfortable, the interviewer knows it's time to probe further.

9. Keep your answers focused on the needs of the organisation.

10. If the question feels inappropriate or sounds unlawful, reframe it by keeping your focus on the requirements of the job.

12

Your questions
CREATING A POWERFUL FINAL IMPRESSION

Asking questions to learn more about the job *and* look good

We've established that an interview is a structured conversation where the interviewer controls the conversation, provides information, and fires questions at you. However, a point should come when you get to ask questions of your own. A professional interviewer will give you this opportunity. You may even be given details of when this will happen – it's usually at the end of the interview. Resist the temptation to jump in earlier.

There is a school of interview coaching which will tell you that an interview is a two-way conversation – the interviewer decides if you fit the role, and you decide whether the organisation is right for you. This really misunderstands what the process is all about. If you use the interview to ask extensive questions, pushing and probing to ensure the job is what you hope, you can easily undermine your chances of a job offer. You can easily sound negative, ultra-cautious, and uncertain if you want the job. The employer may not offer it to you simply because it seems likely you will turn it down.

Forget the idea that it's a two-way conversation or an honest exchange of views. Staff responsible for recruitment are often under pressure to fill roles, and they frequently make them sound as interesting as possible, so deliberately 'sell' the organisation to candidates. You may hear most about attractive aspects of the job, and not very much about the difficult or uninspiring components. You may be presented a biased or incomplete picture of the organisation. This is why you'll do your background checks later. Equally, the people in the room may not be the people you'll be working with – you'll probably want to meet others (such as your line manager or team members).

So, an interview is a *one-way* process. In the room itself you have one goal – *to get close to a job offer*. Don't even try to decide if you want the job while you are there – assume that you do, and make your enthusiasm clear. You're much better off performing what accountants call 'due diligence' outside the room. In fact, even the question 'Do I want the job?' is irrelevant until you have a job offer and all the terms are laid out in writing. Until that's in your hand, keep sending positive messages, and research behind the scenes. Even if you're offered the job on the day, you have plenty of time to do this. If you take a chance to look at job content carefully you're far more likely to make a good decision. Besides, if you decide you want the job, you may have things you want to negotiate (see Chapter 13).

Don't ask basic job-related questions in the interview which you should be discovering for yourself. You'll waste valuable exposure time asking about things that are relatively trivial (and readily accessible) such as the organisation's mileage rate or whether the office is closed between Christmas and New Year. Are these questions what you want to be remembered for after you've left the room?

★Q113   Do you have any questions for us?

At this point in the interview too many candidates politely say, *'No, you've covered everything in great detail, thank you.'*

Wrong answer! Say this, and interviewers feel that your main motivation is getting out of the interview room.

Prepare three or four great questions for this moment. You will probably only use two at the end, but it pays to have reserve questions in case topics come up naturally during the interview itself. Write your questions down before the meeting. Practise saying the actual words out loud. Keep your questions short and simple – a long and complicated question stalls the process.

Q114   Is there anything you'd like to add?

Professional interviewers frequently invite candidates to add important additional details at the end of the interview. This could be a good opportunity to clarify a range of factors:

- an earlier question which you now feel you didn't answer completely
- anything you feel your answers didn't cover in sufficient depth
- a reiteration of your strongest points
- vital additional evidence which hasn't yet been mentioned

The final point is the most important. The most powerful and yet simplest tool you can learn is to analyse an employer's top five or six requirements, and then match them to your strengths. So, at this final stage of the interview, you should be keeping score. If you haven't yet got your top five or six major points across, now is the time to do it – *whether this question is asked or not.* This question is a gift opportunity, but if it isn't asked, create an opportunity to get your answer across anyway. For example, you can thread in a short statement if you're asked if you have any questions for the interviewer:

'Yes, just one point. I believe you're looking for developed negotiation skills, so perhaps I could just say a bit about my training as a mediator. . .'

An interviewer's job is to conclude the interview on time, having covered the key areas. Your job is to make sure you don't leave the interview room without getting across your key messages. If you've done your preparation, you shouldn't be in any doubt about your key points – they should match the shortest version of the employer's shopping list. Even if you can only get two or three points across, don't leave the room until you have.

Closing moments convince

Interviewers pay particular attention to your questions at the end of an interview. They are difficult to predict, so the interviewer needs to pay attention. Smart, intelligent questions show you really understand the job and the organisation. They are the **last event of the interview** so they stick in an interviewer's memory more efficiently than things you said earlier.

The questions you ask at the end of the interview therefore have one purpose only: to give you a final opportunity to shine. We looked at the effect of first impressions in Chapter 4. The final things you say will also have a lasting impact, particularly if you are the last candidate of the day.

So, before you ask any closing questions, **say something positive** about the role. That's because there's a chance that the overall message behind your question is that you are not sure whether you want the job or not. At this stage, this could be a reason to exclude you. Ask your questions, but preface them with a positive comment:

'First of all, I'd like to say how interesting this job sounds. I just want to clarify one or two things. . .'

'I've got some ideas about developing this department, but before pitching them in I'd just like to ask you how you see its future. . .'

'I've a number of useful contacts in the publishing business. How would you feel about extending our consultancy services to that sector?'

'One thing I'd really like to add to this role is the prospect of building up a formal mentoring programme. How would you feel about that?'

The interview may be the only face-to-face meeting you'll get with key decision makers in the organisation, so only pitch questions which reveal you in the best light. So, for example, ask about how the role might develop:

- *'How far would I be responsible for bringing in new business?'*
- *'What training and learning opportunities are available?'*
- *'When would I be able to start writing my own reports?'*

You might, particularly for a senior job, probe the job content to some extent. Don't confuse this with negotiating an adjustment to job content; if that matters to you, do it after the job is offered. Questions about the role balance now are really used to show that you understand what is required for the job holder to be successful – for example:

- *'When do you plan to switch to centralised accounting?'*
- *'Do you anticipate further acquisitions in the next 12 months?'*
- *'I note that you will be appointing two new directors soon. When those roles are filled, what will be the reporting mechanism?'*
- *'Do you expect your sales boom to continue into the next quarter?'*
- *'Who exactly controls the marketing budget?'*
- *'When is this project likely to come on line, and what happens if it doesn't?'*
- *'Given time, I'd be really interested in helping out with planning the annual conference. Do you think I might be able to have some role in that?'*

Whether or not you ask these questions in the room depends on the number of buying signals the interviewer is giving – and how easy it will be to gain access to this person after the interview. If you feel that the job is almost a perfect fit but needs a little tailoring, you may get a chance to raise one question about job content during the interview, particularly if it is a second interview and you feel you are a strong candidate:

'How open would you be to me delegating some of the process parts of this job and initiating some new projects to add to the income stream?'

Pitfalls when asking questions

There are risks in asking questions, which is why you prepare them carefully rather than improvising in the room, which is always dangerous. Making things up on the spur of the moment leads to inane and predictable questions (*'What's the salary?'*) or difficult questions which grind the interview to a halt. If you don't have any questions at all, this sends one message: *'I have very little interest in the job, please allow me to go home.'*

A couple of really strong, well-prepared questions for the final moments of the interview get you a large tick on the interviewer's checklist. These closing seconds of the interview have almost as great an impact as first impressions, and will certainly be remembered. So, think of the invitation for your questions as your **sound bite moment**: the short audio clip that will still be running through the interviewer's head when you are travelling home.

Planning your final questions

You won't get the chance to ask more than a couple of questions at the end of an interview. If one or two pop up during the meeting, take your cue from the interviewer as to the topic. Your main chance is, however, at the end, and the main purpose of your questions is **message reinforcement not information gathering**.

Questions you might ask as the interview draws to a close

There are four kinds of questions that are appropriate at the end of the interview, either because they have a strong impact or because they provide you with useful information:

1) **Questions seeking facts not in the public domain**, for example, with a small or new organisation:
   - *'When did you move into direct marketing?'*
   - *'What platform do you use for your IT?'*

2) **Questions that ask about the future of the job**
   - *'How is the job likely to change in the next couple of years?'*
   - *'What learning opportunities is this job likely to offer?'*
   - *'What kinds of clients would I be working with?'*

3) **Questions that focus on the challenge of the job**
   - *'What kind of results would you expect me to achieve in the first six months?'*
   - *'When would I be able to go on my first client visit?'*
   - *'Can you tell me how much your marketing campaign will draw on social media?'*

These questions are about the future of the role. They communicate your serious interest in the job, and provide vital insights into the role. They show you understand the job and the organisation. However, they do something even more important: they create a strong picture in the interviewer's mind – *you doing the job*.

Once the interviewer has a strong mental image of you working in the role, it's difficult to shake it off. This could make the difference between being number two and number one on the shortlist.

4) *Questions to check next steps*

You have reached the end of the interview. If it has gone well you have communicated a clear series of points about the way your strengths match the requirements of the job. You have thanked the interviewer for his or her time, and you are being walked back to the reception area to pick up your coat.

You may be wondering what happens next. If the interview was set up by a recruitment agency, don't worry – it's the recruitment consultant's job to keep a handle on the process. They will encourage an employer to come to a decision, so all you have to do is to say how you feel the interview went, then ask the consultant what happens next. A recruitment consultant will always ring an employer to ask how the interview went and how you came across – so you should receive some feedback at this point. This may be just words of encouragement, or you may get concrete advice, shaping your future interview performance.

If the employer is filling the job directly, try to get clarity about the next steps in the process before you leave the building. When will the interviews finish? Is there a second round of interviews? When will the final decision be taken? Usually this becomes clear when you ask: *'Can you just let me know what the next stage is, and when the decision will be made?'* If you don't hear within the promised time period, allow a day's grace, and then ring up to ask how things stand. Try to sound friendly and curious, like a fellow professional wondering if a colleague has solved a problem yet, rather than a disgruntled customer who hasn't received a letter.

Q115   Is there any reason you wouldn't take this job?

If you have reservations, now is **not** the time to raise them:

'My only obstacle is that I'm on three months' notice. I'd love to start here right away.'

If you are pressed, for example, as to what aspects of the role you might like to change, you should still be careful. As far as this interview is concerned, the job on offer should seem pretty close to ideal. Try this:

'I see this position as a clear opportunity and the organisation as one I would be proud to join. I don't have any reservations – it all sounds very interesting.'

Or, if the job has obvious drawbacks which it would be naive not to mention:

'I suppose some people might be put off by the travelling involved, but that's one of the attractive aspects as far as I'm concerned.'

Or use this as an opportunity to ask one of the questions you have ready to ask about the job:

'No reservations, just a question – how long before I'd be handling my own accounts?'

Q116   Are you ready to resign? How will you react to a counter-offer?

Recruitment consultancies report that they see talented candidates who progress through several interviews and receive job offers, and then inexplicably turn them down. Detailed questioning usually reveals that they weren't really ready to move on, and hadn't thought carefully about making a change. Sometimes they decided that the job on offer wasn't what they were looking for, but often it's because they were not ready to face the insecurity of a job move – or they aren't sure what they really want. Candidates sometimes apply for jobs just to 'test the water', or they are 'fishing' to see what salary they might command.

Organisations often experience difficulties retaining talented staff. If you announce your departure, your employer may make a counter-offer to persuade you to stay. This might be a pay rise, but could include a promotion, role enhancement, or new learning opportunities. Your employer wants to retain your skills, and it may be cheaper for an employer to offer you something rather than face the disruption of recruiting your replacement.

Expect an interviewer to probe hard about counter-offers. Most people in the recruitment industry believe that anyone who accepts a *financial* counter-offer from their current employer will move on anyway within 12 months. That's because a financial counter-offer doesn't deal with underlying problems.

'With current budget restraints I think a pay rise is unlikely, but it wouldn't alter my decision. I know it's time to move on because the role isn't stretching me any more and there's nothing my employer can do to change that.'

Some agencies press further, asking how you feel about writing a resignation letter. You may not have thought about what resigning from a job will feel like – especially that moment when you see your boss's reaction. If you go pale when this question is asked, you show an interviewer that you're a window shopper who won't commit. An interviewer wants to see that your motivation to change jobs is genuine, and you're not taking interviews just to check your market worth:

'I'd state very simply that I had enjoyed my time with the company and was moving on to new things. And I'd thank them for giving me a really interesting opportunity.'

Think before you are asked – what will you regret about leaving your present job? This question probes whether you are serious about making a change, and you've thought it through. It can give you a good opportunity to reframe your career story while talking about skills and enthusiasm that will transfer:

'Naturally I would really like to take the e-business project to conclusion. However, your investment in e-business is one of the things that really appeals to me about this job. . .'

Q117　What other organisations are interested in you?

Employers like job applicants who are marketable, but they also want to feel they are your first choice. It's best not to mention specific employers; you may mention the wrong kind of organisation (too small, too traditional. . .). However, it does no harm to say that you're in conversation with other companies, but nothing is 'official' yet. Being specific about other roles or organisations may make it sound as if you are balancing competing offers. So avoid naming names:

'I'm having early stage conversations about roles which are not openly advertised, so it would be a breach of trust to say more at this stage.'

This question does at least acknowledge the fact that you have market value. If you say that you have no other irons in the fire it can sound as if you are overdependent on this job. If the interview is with an employer of choice, you might get away with:

'Nothing at the moment, because I have given my entire focus to getting an interview here.'

'I'm in conversation with a couple of organisations at the moment, but we're still some way off a decision. Which suits me, because this is the role I am really interested in. . .'

Q118 We'd like to offer you the job, but we have some concerns. . .

You're close to a job offer, but something stands in the way. Pause, ask for clarification, and listen to these concerns carefully without interrupting to set out a defence. Handle the moment tactfully – you could be one piece of information away from clinching the deal.

'I am happy to talk to you about areas of my experience which will hopefully reassure you on these important points.'

Keep showing enthusiasm. If all else fails, reiterate your top strengths and throw in a sweetener:

'So I believe I have most of the things you're looking for, and as far as the other elements are concerned, my track record shows how quickly I can pick things up in a new role.'

Q119 Can we contact your current employer for a reference?

Clarify exactly when references will be taken and who will be approached. Normally you would only wish your *current* employer to be approached if you have a firm job offer.

'I will be very pleased to provide a reference from my current employer if a position is offered. I assume you'll let me know before taking up any references?'

The exact stage when references are obtained varies considerably. Sometimes it's before shortlisting; sometimes it's after the interview. Be clear about timing, and only provide the names of referees when asked. (Don't just list referees on your CV – you need to know when they will be approached, so you can re-establish contact with referees and tell them why the role interests you).

If it's a general request to take up references from people other than your current employer, your response should be simple and uncomplicated: *'No problem.'* When you get home you may want to call referees to encourage them to respond swiftly. Tell them about the job you're chasing, and tell them why you think the role is a good match.

Q120 When could you start?

The employer is starting to imagine you in the job. Now we really are close to an offer. If you haven't discussed your notice period, do so now with as much flexibility as possible:

'When would you like the new postholder to be in place?'

'Like most people at my level I'm on three months' notice, but I would do what I can to persuade my present employer to release me early once I'd done a good handover.'

Note the subtle difference between 'When could you start?' (tentative, talking about possible futures) and 'When can you start?' (pretty much saying the job is yours).

Questions at the end of the interview not to ask

- **Don't** ask questions that show that you have little idea what the job is about.
- **Don't** ask questions that could have been answered by five minutes spent looking at the company website: for example: *'What is your most successful product?'*, *'How many people work here?'*, *'How many offices do you have?'*
- **Don't** ask about how flexible the company may be on pay. This is the wrong moment, and could provide a reason to exclude you. Deal with this if, and when, you're offered the job.
- **Don't** ask a complicated question that the interviewer will find difficult to answer fairly quickly.
- **Don't** push things too far on job content or flexibility. Ask about that when the employer has decided they can't live without you.
- **Don't** ask questions which raise new problems, for example: *'How would you feel about me working on a job share basis?'*

- ■ **Don't** be smart, ironic, or try to get your own back for all the probing, difficult, fantasy, or unethical questions early on.
- ■ **Don't** ask for special consideration, apologise, or beg.

13

Towards the finishing line

HANDLING A JOB OFFER – OR CONTINUING YOUR SEARCH

Should you follow up if the interview goes brilliantly?

The interview went well and you're pretty sure the job is a great match for your skills and experience. You're optimistic, and waiting to hear the result. Is there anything you can you do right now to increase the chances of a job offer?

If you frequently need to email after an interview to provide vital information, your interview preparation lacks focus. Decide which key points you are going to make – have bullet points written out. Run a mental checklist before the interview concludes. Have you hit the centre of the target enough times? However, there's no such thing as a perfect interview, and you may have missed something under pressure, or you think of a better answer while driving home. Should you call to provide extra information?

Giving yourself some extra edge after an interview is possible, but it takes style and skill. Too often it can sound like you're pushing for a decision, asking for special consideration – both are especially irritating for busy interviewers. If you're told that a hiring decision is going to be made within 24 hours there may be no need to reinforce a good interview, but a friendly email does no harm – ideally one that throws in one small, but important, piece of evidence. If the process is more extended, maintain your visibility by getting in touch, even if it's just to say thank you. Even hardened interviewers like to think that the process has gone well, so if you want to follow up, say '*I know you've got more candidates to see but I just wanted to thank you for a really enjoyable meeting.*' Say why the interview was a good experience. A handwritten card helps – it says something about the time and care you've put into your response.

It's a judgement call – is this overselling, or a useful way of re-establishing contact? Are you ticking an empty box, or throwing in more material in the hope that some sticks? If you really have missed something vital, get in touch – as long as it's a piece of your experience which matters. If you're aiming at a target you've already hit, think again. Mentioning things that are only vaguely relevant sounds like unwelcome persuasion to swing the decision in your favour.

Think about *how* you introduce extra evidence. It should sound conversational, useful, and practical rather than exerting leverage. Another way of reconnecting is to communicate something which has nothing to do with the job. Maybe something came up during the conversation and you have some helpful information you can pass on as a follow-up. Perhaps make a phone call to say '*Thanks again for an enjoyable interview. I'm just about to email a copy of the article I mentioned.*' Any obvious pressure you exert will usually be counterproductive or make you sound desperate for *a* job, not well equipped for *this* job.

So, if you reconnect before a job offer, don't plead or pile on new data; just add one or two highly relevant points, and otherwise say thanks for an enjoyable 'discussion' or 'meeting' – note the subtle avoidance of the word *interview*. Suggesting that it was a gathering of like-minded people reinforces the idea that you're already part of the family.

Edging your way towards a job offer

You've undertaken an effective job search and conducted yourself well in the interview. You've managed not to talk yourself out of the job. You've probably received a number of strong 'buying signals' from the decision maker (talking about the future, picturing you in the role, telling you why you are a good match, asking when you can start). Now you're close to a job-offer conversation, which may happen in the room or, more likely, by telephone shortly afterwards.

Questions for the job offer stage

Take time to think about the job that's being offered to you. Here are some questions – some to reflect on, some to put to other people.

1 **Does this job add to my CV?**
   This is, of course, a question to ask yourself: Will this job enhance your CV? How will it help the way you present yourself to a recruiter in five years' time? Have you done this kind of job before? If so, what's new about it? Does the job title have the right gravity? (If not, this may be something you try to negotiate.)

2 **What parts of the offer do I want to negotiate?**
   Work out what matters to you most from the long list of things that candidates regularly include in

the deal at this stage – money, flexible working, leave, relocation or travel packages, start date, location, pension, health benefits, car, even job content. The important thing to realise is that you can only ask for leverage on a maximum of one or two points, otherwise it sounds as if you are being difficult. Secondly, never try to renegotiate something you have previously agreed as this is seen as unprofessional and can cause the whole deal to collapse.

3 **What have they seen in me that has prompted a job offer?**
We're moving towards questions you will think about asking the employer. If you're unsure what the role is all about you should certainly be seeking more information before acceptance. Asking a question along these lines (try *'I'm really pleased to be offered the job. What made me your first choice?'*) draws out what they see in you, and also expectations. The reasons you've been hired are closely linked to what the organisation sees as success. Appreciating your perceived value may help with salary negotiation (see below).

4 **Can I meet the team?**
While you're considering the details of a written job offer, ask for an opportunity to visit the organisation again (see **Visiting the workplace again before you accept the role** below).

5 **What's the total package?**
Once a clear financial offer is on the table, look at it carefully. If it includes a generous pension and perhaps even some health insurance, that's worth

a lot. If it's a basic salary topped up by bonuses, find out about past bonus expectations and what was paid out. If the pay includes commission, do your homework on how realistic it is to hit the targets set.

6 Can we move the salary offer up a notch?
While job-hunting you should ideally have gained a sense of the salary range for the job. Your aim is to negotiate something on the top 20 per cent or so of this range. Don't be afraid to ask for an improved offer – it will probably cost an employer more to re-advertise and rethink than it will to improve the offer by up to 10 per cent. Stick to your guns, but make it clear at the same time that you're really pleased to be offered the job.

7 How about flexible working?
Rather than pressing on salary you might want to push on additional elements, such as the ability to work from home sometimes. It's much easier to negotiate this now before putting ink on paper. If this is important to you, make it part of the deal you're accepting.

8 Can we look again at role content?
If you feel there is any possibility that you can tweak the job description so that it suits you better, try including this as part of the 'deal'.

9 What results are you looking for in the short term?
It's good to get a clear sense of how you'll be judged in the first three months of starting the role. Ask about preferred outcomes, and what's expected of you, so you don't face any unpleasant surprises down the line.

10 How will the job change?
You're probably hoping that the role offers scope for development and growth. Don't leave that to chance – ask now about opportunities and challenges that will be sent in your direction.

Evaluating and negotiating the job offer

If an offer's on the table, look at it carefully before saying a final and absolute 'yes'. This does *not* mean being difficult or sounding uncertain. It's just about thoroughly examining the deal on the table – not just money; all aspects of the job. For example, as the above questions show, this might be a good time to clarify what you will actually be doing in the job. You won't have the same leverage for another 18 months or so – until you've proved yourself. So if there are important changes to be argued and you feel the employer will be receptive to discussing job content, ask for a conversation.

This process is a matter of comparing two wish lists: what you want in your next career move and what an employer is looking for. A good match means success for both parties; a poor match means an underperforming employee, another career transition, and an unhappy employer. Use the **Job Offer Checklist** below to check out what the deal includes, and which parts you find most acceptable.

This checklist may reveal important things you don't yet know about the job. It also makes it easier for you to tell the difference between items which are deal-breakers, and the things you can live with. Don't expect everything to have a score of two or three – some elements may not be absolutely right for you.

Job Offer Checklist	
Give each factor a score as follows: N Not relevant to me X Poor match to my wish list ✓ Fair match to my wish list ✓✓ Good match to my wish list	
Location	Team fit
Size of organisation	Work sector
Commuting distance	Relationship with boss
Cost of travel to work	Base salary
Public transport route	Bonus scheme/profit sharing
Relocation costs	Period of review
Opportunities for travel	Car/car allowance
Crèche facilities	Pension plan
Working hours	Subsidised loans
Flexible working	Holiday entitlement
Home working	Private health scheme
Impact on my CV	Promotion prospects
Variety	Status, responsibility, authority
Job security	Sports or social facilities
Learning and development opportunities	Organisational culture and values
Extending my network	Community involvement
Other (define your own)	

What matters is the overall balance: are you getting high scores on the things that matter? You're not after the perfect job, and you can only negotiate a few points, not the whole package. If you have already pushed hard on money, for example, you are unlikely to win on other points as well. However, if you have asked for a better pay deal and this has not been accepted, an employer may then be flexible on other factors which cost little to provide.

Visiting the workplace again before you accept the role

You will inevitably have further questions about the job and the organisation which need to be resolved before you come to a final decision. The interview should not be the last opportunity you will have to gather critical information. Too many candidates feel that the only time they are allowed to ask questions about the job is during the selection process. Far from it. Begin with desk research – the 'due diligence' outlined in Chapter 12. Add conversations to the mix as well. One of the best ways of doing this is to spend some time with the people you will actually be working with.

If you get a job offer, it's perfectly reasonable to ask to go back for a second visit while the written job offer is being drafted (this can take more than a week, as there are often key elements to be signed off). Ask to spend a couple of hours with the team you will be joining. This request confirms your strong interest in the job, but also helps you to be sure about accepting the job offer. If this is not convenient (perhaps the team rarely comes together in one place), consider asking for a meeting with your boss.

This confirms your strong interest in the job, but also helps you to be sure that you will fit in, and tells you a great deal about organisational culture. A relaxed workplace visit can tell you a great deal about working style – and you may discover why the last postholder left! Don't risk sounding uncommitted by asking questions which sound as if you're doubtful. Just get people to talk to you about the role. Use the opportunity to find out more about where the organisation is going, where the job fits into the bigger picture, and (ask carefully) what gets in the way of success.

When you make the request, make sure it doesn't sound as if you're getting cold feet about the offer:

'I'm really thrilled about the job offer. I look forward to receiving the paperwork. While it's being sorted out I'd really like the opportunity to meet up with the actual team to get to know people. Next week would be good for me. . .'

If the company sounds unsure, explain that you're really interested in the role and want to find out more about the challenges ahead. Your suggested visit may not be possible for reasons of security or confidentiality of information, but if the organisation turns down your suggestion for any other reason, you might wonder what is being hidden from sight.

Q121 How does this job compare with others you are applying for?

It's easy to fall into the trap of hinting that there are other jobs out there that are more attractive. On the other hand, giving the impression that this is the only job on your radar smacks of desperation. The unasked questions here are 'How marketable are you?' and 'How committed are you to this specific job?' There is a simple rule here. Leave the interviewer in no doubt that this job is your number one choice. A broad comparison here will easily pitch things in your favour:

'For me, this position is much more interesting than others I've looked at because. . .'

Then go on to say why this job and this company appeal to you *and* why the role is a great match for your skill set.

Q122   The job is yours. I assume you're OK with the standard package?

Some employers like to close the deal in the room with a verbal job offer. The danger here is that you are so overwhelmed by good news that judgement goes out of the window, and you blurt out a quick 'yes'. Don't be flattered into accepting the job on the spot without considering the offer terms. You can only do this quietly, outside the interview room.

Choose the tone of your answer with care. Avoid sounding suspicious or undercommitted, but do ask for time to think about the offer (and decide on a negotiation strategy if one is required). Top and tail your comments with positive remarks:

'I'm delighted with your offer. I really enjoyed our discussion and I know I am really going to enjoy this job. Can you give me a day or so to have a look through the details of your written offer? As for a start date – I'm on three months' notice, but I will see what I can do. I really want to get on with it!'

Q123   What's your current salary?

Tread carefully. There are three key issues here:

- Did you mention your salary in a covering letter or an application form? If so, be consistent – give a factual answer, but follow it up with a clear statement of intent: *'I'm paid £XX, but am looking for a salary that reflects my skills and experience.'*
- If you are paid more than the job on offer: *'I fully recognise that this will be a pay cut, but this is a role that really interests me. . .'*
- If you are paid significantly less than the job on offer: *'This job would be a pay rise for me – exactly what I can't get in my present role.'*

★Q124   What sort of pay figure did you have in mind?

(a) Answering this question during the interview process
This question can come up at any stage. Have one aim from the start: **keep off the topic of pay until you have been given a job offer**. If the issue comes up earlier, avoid detailed discussion without having a real sense of the value of the role – what problems does it solve? How eager is the employer to fill the job quickly? Naming a figure early can be problematic: too high, and you may rule yourself out early in the process; too low, and you may suggest you're not up to the job.

If pressed, start by asking what the salary range is for similar positions in the organisation, and then continue to talk about a range rather than a specific figure. Once you have a job offer on the table, you have far more negotiating power. If you state a figure you are prepared to accept, you have lost all room for manoeuvre. So if the question is raised early in the process, always try to get the employer to shoot first:

'What salary range is on offer?'

Do your homework: research the likely pay range by looking at job advertisements, talking to recruitment agencies and industry contacts. Work out what the top 20 per cent of earners in this kind of role are earning, and try to get a feel for what a 'top 20 per cent' candidate would look like. What evidence and image do you need to offer to get an offer in that pay range?

If you are pressed at this early stage on what pay level would be acceptable, don't talk about the figure you would 'settle' for, and definitely do not say you expect to receive a lower salary. If the employer believes you can do the job, they should believe you will be good value at some point above the middle of the employer's pay range. Having decided on you, an employer doesn't want to go to the trouble of rethinking the selection process. A tried and tested way is to pitch yourself towards the top half of the anticipated pay range and say:

'I'm being interviewed for jobs paying in the range. . .'

(b) **Answering this question at the job offer stage**
You're in a much better position answering this question when you hold a job offer – ideally in writing with an employer firmly committed. Now you have some power. You won't have this much leverage until you've been in the job for over a

year – possibly longer. At this moment an employer wants to reel you in and close the file. This doesn't mean you'll get anything or everything you ask for. However, it is fairly common for candidates to negotiate something at this stage, and employers respect this.

What will you negotiate? Avoid saying 'yes' too early. Work out what matters to you most from the long list of things that candidates regularly include in the deal at this stage: money, flexible working, leave, relocation or travel packages, start date, location, pension, health benefits, car, even job content (see the **Job Offer Checklist** on page 225). The important thing to realise is that you can negotiate no more than one or two points, otherwise it sounds as if you are being difficult. Never try to renegotiate something you have previously agreed as this is seen as unprofessional. Use softening-up questions:

'Is there any flexibility at the top end of the range?'

'Bearing in mind that I'm being interviewed for positions paying more than your offer, what flexibility is there?'

'Taking account of bonuses and other payments, my current salary is only just a margin below what you're offering. It would be good to feel that this was a real step forward. . .'

Or use one of a range of classic negotiation tactics:

'From what I know of the marketplace, I believe good people in this field are earning rather more

than your offer. I think I'm worth a higher salary because of what I'd bring to your business. . .'

'I realise you need to keep costs under control, but do bear in mind that I'll make a significant difference to your overall income. We're discussing a salary difference of £5,000 a year, and I could easily be bringing in that much extra income on a monthly basis.'

'In your shoes I'd be watching my staffing costs too. However, I intend to provide you cost savings 20 times higher than my salary. . .'

'We're just £2,000 apart. That's about £40 a week. You spend that kind of money on refills for the water cooler. . .'

When you ask for something different or something to be added to the deal, remember how important it is to *keep on sounding enthusiastic.* Use the **happy sandwich** technique: your request begins and ends with really strong messages that confirm that you are on board:

'I really enjoyed the interview and I'm thrilled to be your first choice. Naturally there are a couple of things I'd like to look at while the paperwork is being drawn up. It would be good to be clear about how many days a week I would need to be in London. I also wonder if you can move the salary up just a little, in line with other roles I've been looking at? If you could squeeze an extra £2,000 out of the budget, that would work for me. I'll leave that with you, but can I say I am over the moon to be offered the job. . .'

Q125 Would you take the job at a lower salary?

You might be asked to take a lower salary than advertised, or a lower salary than you're expecting. This is a
difficult question for any candidate. You've got the job,
but the cash-strapped employer is changing the terms.
Be careful that you don't give too much away too soon.
Again, start positive, but hold your ground:

*'I'm delighted you're offering me the job. However, a
salary below the advertised range won't work for me. I
hope I've demonstrated that I will be a good return on
investment, and if we can just get the pay level right
we can close the deal very quickly, I'm sure.'*

Buying time allows you to think about a negotiation
strategy, and also how much you want the job. If the
employer is entirely inflexible on salary, ask for a day
to consider and come back with alternatives such as
an earlier-than-normal review date, or perhaps other
elements that you might negotiate in the job.

Staying resilient – job searching after rejection

If you don't get a job offer, you may feel disheart-
ened. Rejection isn't an easy thing to deal with in
the job-hunting process. Take some time out doing
things which have nothing to do with applying for
jobs, and then look at the situation objectively. You
may take a few days to get your confidence back.
The day you receive a rejection letter is not a good
day to be rewriting your CV or trying to network with
new people.

If you have got to the shortlist stage, this is pretty good evidence that you can do the job. If someone was appointed who has slightly better skills or experience, that means the selection process was undertaken properly. Final decisions beyond the shortlist are often made on the basis of personality and cultural fit, and as long as you came across as confident, open, and friendly, there is not much more you can do. Remember that you can't control all the factors in the process.

Don't give up. Job interviews are like sales outings: a number of people have to say 'no' before somebody says 'yes'. Here's a phrase you might like to write on the folder where you keep copies of job applications: **rejection is not feedback**. Much of the time rejection is not about you at all – selection decisions are made for all kinds of reasons, some of them fairly arbitrary – particularly when it comes to shortlisting.

Do try, however, to get some proper, helpful feedback on your interview performance. Some candidates ask for this as if they have a right to receive it, but they don't. An employer doesn't have to get back to unsuccessful candidates, and is very unlikely to give you detailed feedback, especially in writing, because you might use that as evidence to challenge the selection decision. So, don't sound like you're asking why you didn't get the job. You're much better off saying you are pleased the employer was able to fill the role, and asking for constructive advice: *'Can you do me a favour and tell me something about the strengths and weaknesses of my interview technique?'* Ask for verbal feedback as it is more likely to be unguarded.

Be warned – most interview feedback you will receive will be bland, generalised and not terribly helpful ('We found someone who matched the role better than you.') Such feedback can easily be counterproductive:

you don't feel good about it, and you haven't learned anything either. Sometimes there are clear, objective reasons you don't get a job, but usually the employer has chosen the person who 'feels' right – something they will never admit. Don't be too worried by unfocused feedback: 'Your examples were a little brief.' The danger is that you over-adjust and miss out vital information next time. Don't tinker with your interview strategy unless you get concrete feedback you can act on.

Remember that interviewers, particularly those working for recruitment agencies, hold strong opinions about interview practice. Some of this is useful, some of it represents personal preferences. Follow a simple rule – if you get similar feedback from several sources (for example, 'You are not communicating your skills in the right language for our sector'), that's tangible feedback you can work with. If you find that you repeatedly don't get beyond first interviews – and feedback doesn't tell you why – seek help so you know which interview behaviours to adjust.

Find someone to coach you through a practice interview. Some faults will be easy for a coach to identify. You might 'um' and 'er', or take too long to think of an answer (unprepared it can take people 20–30 seconds to come up with a reasonable answer to a high-level question). Perhaps you use the same phrase repeatedly. You might speak too quietly or drop to an undertone at the end of each answer. You might lose track of questions. Get someone to review the way you dress, sound, and how you come across in the opening moments, looking again at Chapter 4 in this book. Practise your answers to tough questions, your lines of defence, and pitching your most important messages.

Address as much as you can in practice – don't use real job interviews to master the basics. And if you are knocked back again, focus on what went well, find someone to encourage you, and keep trying. You may have to attend several interviews and experience multiple rejections – but it only takes one job offer for choices to open up for you.

WHAT TO DO IF YOU DON'T GET THE JOB

A 10-step guide to pulling yourself up by your bootstraps

1. Learn from your interview experience. Ask for **feedback** by telephone (the company is very unlikely to spell out their recruitment decision-making process in writing).
2. Focus on **what went well** in the interview, and build on it.
3. Work out **what you would do differently** if you have a similar interview next time.
4. If you intend to go for other jobs in the same industry, get some more **practice**.
5. Practise answers to **difficult questions** which leave you floundering.
6. Work hard on pre-packaging your **evidence**.
7. Compose your **Safety Zone Responses**. Write them down.
8. Revisit your work history for better and clearer evidence of your **competencies**.
9. Are you still interested in the job? If so, write a warm **thank-you note**. It's not too rare that the top candidate drops out after the job offer stage. You could still be in the frame.
10. Work on your technique. An interview is a **performance**. Good performances need practice to become great.